How to Study the Qur'an:
Sayyid Abul Hasan Ali Nadwi's Approach

Ahsan Academy of Research
(Springs, South Africa)

How to Study the Qur'an:
Sayyid Abul Hasan Ali Nadwi's Approach

Abdul Kader Choughley

Tawasul International
Centre for Publishing, Research and Dialogue

First Edition 2021
Second Edition 2024
ISBN: 978-93-90167-85-2

Abdul Kader Choughley

Ahsan Academy of Research (Springs, South Africa) info@ahsanacademy.co.za
www.ahsanacademy.co.za

Tawasul International
Centre for Publishing, Research and Dialogue
(Rome, Italy)

CONTENTS

Acknowledgements

I am pleased to announce that the present work is a revised edition of Sayyid Abul Hasan Ali Nadwi contributions to Qur'anic studies. It has been an engagingly productive time to offer a balanced, nuanced interpretation of the sacred text.

A number of friends have encouraged me to take on this responsibility of sharing my thoughts about the 'ulama's contributions to Qur'anic studies. The choice of Shaykh Nadwi is a positive approach to locate the merger between traditional and contemporary Qur'anic sources.

My mentor, the late Dr Yusuf Bamjee stood out for his exemplary devotion to the sacred text. His activist contribution to make the Qur'an a timeless source of guidance of Muslim collective life is best represented in Ahsan Academy's widely-acclaimed publications.

Another friend, Omar Essop has been instrumental in sustaining our multivolume project by his encouragement and moral support.

In the preparation of this work the collaborative support of Akhtar Husein Seedat may be mentioned. His commitment to promoting the Qur'anic message in a contemporary setting is one of his outstanding attributes. I consider it an honour to be associated with him in our quest of sharing the gems of Qur'anic wisdom to the modern mind.

I owe a great debt of gratitude to my wife, Muniera for her editorial and technical production of the volume. Finally, our sincere appreciation to our donors and well-wishers who have made this publication possible.

Abdul Kader Choughley
(Springs: South Africa)
04 February 2021

In the name of Allah, Most Compassionate, Most Merciful

Foreword

Dr Abdul Kader Choughley is widely acclaimed for his perceptive writings on modern South Asian Islam, especially on the sterling contribution of the illustrious Muslim scholar, Sayyid Abul Hasan Ali Nadwi (1913-1999). Recently Dr Choughley delivered a stirring and valuable lecture on Shaykh Nadwi's contribution to Qur'anic Studies at the K. A. Nizami Centre for Qur'anic Studies, Aligarh Muslim University on 04 October 2017 at Aligarh, India. The present work stands out as a brilliant elaboration of his substantial Lecture.

Shaykh Nadwi whom Dr Choughley lovingly refers to as Shaykh Nadwi, ranks as a leading 20th century Muslim scholar. His authoritative exposition of Islam couched in the best profound Islamic intellectual and spiritual traditions, went a long way in revitalizing Muslims' faith in the Islamic way of life. His writings appearing originally in Arabic and Urdu, which were avidly translated into other languages of the Muslim world, account in a large measure, for emergence and consolidation of the phenomenon of Islamic resurgence in the late 20th century. Shaykh Nadwi was conferred with the prestigious Shah Faisal Award for his laudable role in Islamic revivalism.

The Qur'an occupies the pivotal place in Shaykh Nadwi's elucidation of things Islamic. He was fortunate enough to assimilate the meaning and message of the Qur'an, first at his home known for piety and scholarship, and later at the feet of such outstanding teachers as Khalil Arab and Mawlana Ahmad Ali Lahori. Shaykh Nadwi drew also upon the writings of Shaykh Ibn Taymiyyah. He benefitted much from his interaction with Shaykh Taqi Al-Din Hilāli.

Throughout his illustrious career, as an Islamic revivalist *par excellence* Shaykh Nadwi displayed his unflinching commitment to the Qur'an. Apart from offering his inspiring and profound interpretation of the meaning and message of the Qur'an, he provided valuable guidance to readers, instructing them how to study of the Qur'an with profit. In one of his laudable pieces he sets out the following prerequisites for a rewarding study of the Qur'an:

How to Study the Qur'an:
Sayyid Abul Hasan Ali Nadwi's Approach

1. One's sincere desire for grasping the Qur'anic message.
2. One's resolve to act on what he learns from the study of the Qur'an.
3. God-consciousness should permeate one's heart and mind while studying the Qur'an.
4. One's firm faith in the Qur'an as the Word of God.
5. One's serious reflection on the Qur'anic contents.
6. One should exert himself both mentally and spiritually in his study.

Conversely, the following traits hinder one from deriving benefits from the study of the Qur'an:

- Arrogance
- Contesting the wisdom of the Qur'an
- One's lack of belief in the doctrine of the Hereafter.

Shaykh Nadwi's main contribution to the Qur'anic studies through his many writings and lectures consist in his brilliant exposition of the message and wisdom of the Qur'an for 20th century man lost in the morass of materialism. Cogently he pressed home the truth how the Qur'anic guidance was articulated by the Messengers of Allah down the ages. He urged fellow Muslims to imbibe the message of the Qur'an in their conduct, which would, in turn, prove highly effective in *da'wah* (call to Islam). In its early days Islam spread far and wide, as the early Muslims were the embodiments of the Qur'anic morals and manners. Even their foes recognized their unblemished character and conduct. Likewise, Muslims should be imbued with unshakable faith, which the Qur'an demands of them. It will bring them the best of both the worlds. Devotional worship being the manifestation of deep faith should be the hallmark of Muslims. It would strengthen their bond with the Qur'an. For all modes of Islamic worship are inseparable from the Qur'an. More importantly, Muslims' social relations, particularly their interaction with non-Muslims should be governed by the Qur'anic teachings. As long as Muslims adhere to the Qur'anic moral code, their individual and collective life will remain exemplary. Their entire way of life, be it political, economic or socio-cultural, should conform to the Qur'anic terms of reference. His much acclaimed book, *Guidance from the Holy Qur'an* (2005) is a testament to his nuanced understanding (*tafsīr*) of the Qur'an.

Dr Choughley has done well to analyse Shaykh Nadwi's enrichment of the field. In doing so, he has delved deep into Shaykh Nadwi's approach to promoting the Qur'an, particularly in the West. Furthermore, his writings brought into sharper focus the Qur'anic epistemology. His tribute to Shaykh Nadwi's genius represents the fruits of his enviable scholarship.

Dr Choughley's works, including the present one, will prove highly beneficial for all those interested in the Islamic resurgence, Qur'anic studies and Islam in the Indo-Pak subcontinent. He deserves accolades for this inspiring work. May Allah shower upon both Shaykh Nadwi and Dr Choughley His choicest blessings.

Professor Abdur Raheem Kidwai
sulaim_05@yahoo.co.in
Aligarh Muslim University Aligarh, India
January 2018

Introduction

The study aims to examine the contributions of Sayyid Abul Hasan Ali Nadwi (d. 1999) to Qur'anic studies. A long and eventful career spanning over seventy years, Shaykh Nadwi is considered a leading scholar in the Islamic resurgence[1] discourse. Noted for his intellectual and biographical writings, Shaykh Nadwi has carved a niche in Qur'anic studies. Although no traditional commentary (*tafsīr*) was written by him, several books on Qur'anic topics and themes underscore his mastery over the foundational text of Islam.

Shaykh Nadwi's profound study of the Qur'an has specific settings, and in many respects sets him apart as an independent scholar committed to the ideals and realities embodied in the Divine scripture.

Formative Influence

Our focus is on the formative influence of the Qur'an in respect of Shaykh Nadwi's intellectual thought and his interpretive reading of its message in a contemporary perspective.

Shaykh Nadwi's extensive study of the Qur'an is reflected in his prolific writings. He was thoroughly grounded in the rich field of Islamic scholarship; his command over the Arabic language provided him with the consummate skills to express forcefully the elegance and subtle meanings of the Qur'an. The following extract reveals the formative period of his role as a Qur'anic scholar:

"After completing my education, I turned my attention again to the study of the Qur'an. I made a point of studying books in addition to the texts prescribed in the *madāris*. In pursuance of this objective, I went to Lahore and studied the whole of the Qur'an at the feet of Mawlana Ahmad Ali Lahori (d. 1962). His total devotion to the Qur'an impressed me most. Whatever he said and did was prompted by the Qur'an. This cast a spell on my heart. His piety, his ascetic way of life and his adherence to the sunnah in every action impressed me much.[2]"

---

[1] Terms like Islamic resurgence and Islamic revivalism are interchangeably used in the book.

[2] Abul Hasan Ali Nadwi, *Guidance from the Holy Qur'ān*. Translated by Abdur Raheem Kidwai (Leicester, 2005), 3.

Lahori was a celebrated exegete whose fame rests on his cogent presentation of the Qur'anic teachings. His Qur'anic approach is reflected by the political activist, Mawlana 'Ubaydullah Sindhi (d. 1944) who developed a theme–based interpretation of the sacred text. Sindhi's extensive tears of exile in Turkey and Makkah opened up new vistas of understanding the Qur'anic worldview.[3]

In his autobiography *Kārwān i-Zindagi*[4], Shaykh Nadwi provides interesting insights into the life and times of Lahori. The erudite 'alim honed Shaykh Nadwi's scholarly profile. His poignant account about obtaining impressive results in the *tafsīr* examination was an a tacit endorsement of Lahori's unflinching faith in his capability as a promising Qur'anic scholar. Furthermore, his correspondence with Lahori[5] was a pointed reference to his overflowing love and affection for Shaykh Nadwi. No doubt, this reciprocal relationship bore unmissable traits of the serious engagement with the broader understanding of *tafsīr* in a sociopolitical milieu. In sum, there were definite emerging patterns of *tafsīr* located in the subcontinent.[6]

The course offered by Lahori was equivalent to a post-graduate programme for 'ulama. It attracted 'ulama from across the subcontinent who rediscovered the treasures of Qur'anic teachings beyond the confines of *madrasah* institutions. Lahori's charisma exuded an aura of spirituality in his lessons; his unique teaching method connected the mind and soul to the divine message of *tawhīd* (Oneness of Allah) and unconditional love for the Holy Prophet (peace be upon him). In sum, the illustrious scholar embodied a quest for knowledge in the field of Qur'anic studies and the reformation of Muslim society. Shaykh Nadwi internalised these positive qualities in his *da'wah* mission.[7]

The sense of independence displayed by Lahori in his interaction with powerful, influential figures features prominently on his anecdotal accounts.[8] For him the Qur'anic injunction of expressing the truth under every circumstance was his badge of honour. Likewise, Lahori did not mix freely with the élite of Punjab. Rather, he would warn them of the divine punishment for their apathy and exploitative behaviour towards the weak,

---

[3] Muhammad Hajjan Shaikh, *Maulana Ubaid Allah Sindhi: A Revolutionary Scholar* (Islamabad, 1986), 255-6.

[4] Nadwi, *Kārwān i-Zindagi*, vol.1, 132-3.

[5] Nadwi, *Purān i-Charāgh*, vol.1, 161-2.

[6] Ibid., 154-5.

[7] Nadwi, *Kārwān i-Zindagi*, vol. I (Lucknow, 1983), 128-32.

[8] See Ahmad Ali Lahori, *Khutbāt i-Lāhori*, 5 volumes (Deoband, 1986).

vulnerable Muslim labourers. His lectures were direct, blunt and forceful that were reflective of his deep study of the Qur'an. There was no compromise in speaking the truth. The élite too, did not utter a word of complaint and lowered their heads out of shame. Lahori belonged to that rare breed of `ulama who were not afraid to raise concerns, and if need be, to criticise those people whose actions were against the shari'ah.

Shaykh Nadwi had an independent mind and developed his own methods of understanding the message of the Qur'an. He was a non-conformist in the sense that he believed that the Qur'an appealed to readers from all facets of life; hence, its universal relevance. As much as he profited from Lahori's classes, he designed an innovative course to meet the intellectual needs of students. Outside the classroom environment, he together with the noted scholar, Mawlana Abdul Salam Kidwai, was actively involved at the Idarah Ta'limat i-Islam.[9] Its primary aim was to impart Qur'anic classes to government officials, professionals and the educated class with an interest in Islamic studies.

Kidwai possessed impeccable academic credentials: lecturer at Nadwah and Jamia Millia Islamia university; editor of *Nadwah* journal and a capable administrator. He is best remembered for his Qur'anic contributions.[10]

The *Ten Lessons of Arabic*[11] enabled students with a modicum knowledge of Islam to gain adequate familiarity with Arabic in order to access directly the meaning and message of the Qur'an. Kidwai adopted a novel approach to integrate his lessons for the modern mind: a simple translation of the verses followed by a concise discussion of grammatical rules. Students were encouraged to attempt a translation of the Qur'anic text to assimilate a direct understanding of its essential teachings and wisdom. Obviously, supervision under a teacher was essential. Based on his lesson-based approach, Kidwai succeeded in stimulating, to a great degree, interest in Qur'anic studies among professionals and ordinary people. Thus, he lent considerable knowledge and expertise to expand the scholarly network for a meaningful engagement with the sacred text.[12]

In the 'ulama tradition, Mawlana Husayn Ahmad Madani (d. 1957)[13] is

---

[9] Nadwi, *Kārwān,* vol. 1, 273-5.

[10] Muhammad Tariq Ayubi, *Nadwi Fuzalii ki Qur'āni Khidmiit* (New Delhi, 2019), 36.

[11] Abu Sufyan Islahi, *Idārah Sir Sayyid Muslim University Aligarh ke Mashāhir i-Qur'āniyiit* (New Delhi,2017), 133-6.

[12] Ayubi, *Nadwi Fuzalā,* 37-8.

[13] For a biographical account on Madani, see Nadwi, *Purān i-Charāgh,* vol. 1 (Karachi, 1984), 96-116.

regarded as a custodian of Islamic teachings in a changing sociopolitical milieu. The dominant discourse in his chequered career was the freedom of the Indian subcontinent from the British colonial rule. His overriding concern for the welfare of the Muslim community also revealed his extraordinary commitment to the cause of Islam.

According to Shaykh Nadwi, Madani had tapped in the reservoirs of Qur'anic and *hadīth* studies; his classes resonated with the critical reading of the primary sources of Islam. Shaykh Nadwi's association with Madani may be viewed from two angles: his knowledge and personal traits. He observes:

"During my stay there, I sought an appointment with Mawlana Madani so as to benefit from his elucidation of some difficult Qur'anic passages. These points were left unresolved in the standard *tafāsir*. Mawlana Madani was one of the distinguished 'ulama of the day. Apart from his expertise in *hadīth* studies and other disciplines, he had carried out an intensive study of the Qur'an. His lifestyle reflected the fruits of his special study. I was fortunate that he granted me time on Fridays to discuss with him such Qur'anic verses as I found hard to fathom. The Mawlana was a frequent traveler and this was a period of hectic political activity. Yet I managed to draw, to some extent, upon his scholarship."[14]

Two outstanding qualities which endeared Shaykh Nadwi to Madani were the latter's unimpeachable sincerity and selflessness (*ikhlās wa be-gharzi*) which he assimilated into his own life. Madani's mission highlighted on a broader level the challenges Indian 'ulama faced in mapping out their future career and also offering alternatives to the realities–social, religious and political–caused by the Partition of India in 1947.[15]

Translocal scholarship was emerging in the nineteenth century in the subcontinent and had a direct bearing on Nadwah. Its influence shaped the future of Nadwah as international institution of Islamic higher learning. The presence of Arab scholars at the institution served as a catalyst for its growing reputation among the *madāris* in the Arab world.

Under the patronage of Shah Jahan Begum and her consort, Nawab Siddiq Hasan Khan, ideologue of the Ahl i-*Hadīth* movement in the subcontinent, many Yemeni scholars settled in the princely state of

---

[14] Nadwi, *Guidance from the Holy Qur'ān*, 3.
[15] Nadwi, *Purān i-Charāgh*, vol. 1, 110-1.

Bhopal.[16] The proliferation of *hadīth* studies spread significantly to major Islamic centres during the early nineteenth century. Essentially, the focus of the salafi tradition embodied an inclusive approach to the study of the foundational sources of Islam.[17] In other words, the Ahl i-*Hadīth* articulation of Islamic authenticity formed the basis of the *tajdīd* (renewal) discourse. This self-belief, however, did not imply that its literalist interpretation was uncritically endorsed in the 'ulama circles. At the other end of the spectrum, reformist thought (*islāh*) was carried out by 'ulama with *tasawwuf* leanings. Thus, the synthesis of tradition and spirituality merged into a distinct Islamic ethos.

In the domain of Qur'anic studies the classical *tafsirs* were representative of trans-local scholarship that were gradually incorporated into the curriculum of *madāris* that were amenable, in some measure to the salafi reformist trends.[18] Again, it was the Yemeni scholars who made their dominant mark in reconfiguring key Qur'anic concepts within the ambit of Islamic authenticity. To this class of 'ulama belonged Khalil Ahmad Yemeni (d. 1966), reverentially addressed as Arab Sahib, who was a paragon of classical Arabic literature and was widely acclaimed as a *mufassir* (Qur'anic commentator). He represented in his personality the following trait described in the *hadīth*: "True faith is embedded in the people of Yemen."[19]

Shaykh Nadwi imbibed the true content of faith in the company of Arab Sahib. He focused on Qur'anic topics relating to *tawhid*. The key theme in his vision was promoting the dimensions of Islam in its pristine form. Shaykh Nadwi recounts Arab Sahib's attachment to the Qur'an and his recitation of specific *surahs* which enraptured the hearts of listeners:

"Not only was he (Arab Sahib) a Qur'anic scholar, he was devoted heart and soul to the Book. Whenever he recited the Book, tears rolled down his cheeks. I was impressed by his mode of recitation which was characterised by pathos. It reinforced the thrust of the Qur'anic passages recited by him. For at numerous places the Qur'an laments man's indifference to the divine message and its resultant loss."[20]

---

[16] See Claudia Preckel, *Begums of Bhopal* (New Delhi, 2000), 125 –9.

[17] Ibid., 127-8.

[18] Nadwah stood out among traditional *madāris* for its pragmatic approach to *tafsir* studies. See Muhammad Mubin Salim, *Model Syllabus for Teaching the Qur'ān in Madrasahs (Aligarh, 2019)*, 17-9.

[19] Arab Sahib's impact on Shaykh Nadwi's scholarship is discussed in Nadwi, *Purān i-Charāgh*, vol. 1, 220.

[20] Nadwi, *Guidance from the Holy Qur'ān*, 2.

According to Shaykh Nadwi, the concept of *tawhid* embodied Arab Sahib's presentation of Islamic teachings. It was an obvious emphasis framed against the backdrop of syncretic practices among Muslims in the subcontinent. The core belief structure (`aqidah) was compromised to the veneration of shrine-based Islam. Shaykh Nadwi focused primarily on *tawhid* and its implication in a Qur'anic perspective.[21] His writings and lectures are a recurrent theme in his articulation of correct `aqidah.

Arab Sahib was an embodiment of the Qur'anic ideal of *da`wah*. Quite often he was invited by organisations and professionals to deliver speeches about the salient features of Islamic teachings. It must be remembered that Arab Sahib was a lecturer at Lucknow University and familiar with the prevalent academic trends. This underscored his ability to interact with a wide array of people from diverse backgrounds.

For Shaykh Nadwi, it was Arab Sahib's attachment to the Qur'an that raised his eminence and popularity. A point in case was his melodious recitation of selected verses from Surah Al-Furqān that struck the emotional chords of listeners. The measured cadence that he deftly employed in his recitation bore the hallmarks of an 'ālim deeply immersed in the oceans of Qur'anic knowledge.[22]

The following extract lucidly explains the powerful influence of *tawhīd* in man's existence:

"When a person acquires correct understanding of *tawhid*, he understands that the entire universe is functioning under a well-managed and well-controlled system and every object of the universe is running in a well-coordinated way. He can easily understand the intricacies and nuances of life. He can build a society on righteousness, piety, justice, tolerance and mutual cooperation. He can overcome all kinds of prejudices. He can view the entire mankind as a single family. He can combine *dīn* (divine religion) and *dunyā* (worldly pursuit) and fulfil the needs of both this life and the Afterlife."[23]

---

[21] On the doctrines of Islam, See Nadwi, *A Guidebook for Muslims* (Lucknow, 1985), 57-78.

[22] Nadwi, *Purān i-Charāgh*, vol.1, 220-1.

[23] Nadwi, *Islam: Three Core Beliefs* (Kuala Lumpur, 2016), 45.

Tafsīr Works of Reformist Scholars

Two luminaries of Qur'anic scholarship have enriched the intellectual discourse on reformist trends across the Muslim world. Apart from their voluminous works, their respective contributions to the *tafsīr* tradition are remarkable for their originality and independent approach.

Ibn Taymiyyah (d. 1328)[24] possessed a profound and analytical mind, an attribute that bore testimony to his versatile genius. His *Muqaddimah*[25] (Introduction) on the principles of *tafsīr* is a synopsis of the correct approach adopted by the *salaf.* By this term he means the earlier generation of Muslim scholars who were not swayed by extremism in approaching the study of the Qur'an. Their interpretive reading was based on the sunnah and the views of the Companions (*Sahābah*) who served as reference point in disseminating the message of the Qur'an. Ibn Taymiyyah also critiqued the *tafsir* works of rationalists and *sufis*, which were at variance with authentic interpretations of the *salaf.*

Shah Waliyullah (d. 1762)[26] is considered an icon in the reform movement in the subcontinent. His long term objective was to revive the paramount position of the Qur'an and sunnah in order to rejuvenate the intellectual life of Muslims. Apart from his Qur'anic translation in Persian, his work on the principles of *tafsīr* is a supplement to an objective understanding of the text. His *Al-Fawz al-Kabir*[27] which is recognised as a standard introduction to *tafsīr* has the following features: a concise treatment of the methodological approaches and brevity of ideas couched in brief comments. According to Shaykh Nadwi, this work is an essential guide which provides new insights into the intellectual appreciation of the Qur'an.

Shaykh Nadwi assiduously studied the above books in order to gain a comprehensive understanding of this important discipline.

---

[24] On the life and times of Ibn Taymiyyah, see Nadwi, *Saviours of Islamic Spirit*, vol. 2 (Lucknow, 1974).

[25] Ibn Taymiyyah, *Muqaddimah i Usul al-Tafsir*, Translated by Abdul Haq Ansari (Birmingham, 1993).

[26] Nadwi, *Saviours of Islamic Spirit*, vol. 4 (Lucknow, 1993); Cf. Mahmood Ghazi, *Islamic Renaissance in South Asia 1707-1867* (Islamabad, 2002).

[27] Shah Waliyyullah, *Al-Fawz al-Kabir i Usul al-Tafsir.* Translated by G.N. Jalbani (Karachi, 1980).

The Qur'anic Perspective: An Overview

During the formative period of his study, Shaykh Nadwi made perceptive observations about the study of the Qur'an. Apart from linguistic proficiency and literary finesse of Arabic, which enables a student to wade through volumes of the *tafsīr* literature, there are other factors that impact the understanding of the message of the Qur'an. Shaykh Nadwi too, pursued *tafsīr* studies in a conventional way: a verbatim reading of multivolume texts. However, this approach did not produce the intimate affinity between the reader and the Divine text. The corpus of *tafsir* literature encompasses a vast horizon of history, literature, philosophy and theology. Even lexicons have made noteworthy contributions to analyse the contextual relevance of words and phrases contained in the Qur'an. In retrospect, there is no dearth of study over the fourteen centuries which has not attempted to unravel the majesty, authenticity and inimitability of the Qur'an.[28] Shaykh Nadwi states unequivocally that a textual relationship does not invariably yield all the responses in terms of meaning. For all practical purposes, the knowledge and tenor of *nabuwwat* (Prophethood) should be embedded in the lives of believers which mirror the following *hadīth*: "The Prophet's character was the Qur'an."

The interplay between word and deed is tersely expressed. The righteous scholars bore traces of the Prophetic temperament in their personal conduct. It was therefore not surprising that the subtle meanings of the Qur'an which were not easily accessible in *tafsīr* literature were highlighted in an informal way through their lectures on Qur'anic themes. For Shaykh Nadwi, it was a vista of new insights which strengthened his understanding of the depth and dynamism of the Qur'an.

Following into the footsteps of the Holy Prophet (peace be upon him) creates new openings for readers to participate in the ebb and changing fortunes of human lives. Visualise, in Qur'anic terminology, the emotional and expressive response of the Prophet (peace be upon him) to specific situations. You will relate heart and soul to the graphic description of incidents mentioned in the Qur'an. A striking picture or scenario emerges from these incidents in which the reader participates orally and visually. The Qur'anic descriptions go beyond morality and enable readers to develop an emotional and spiritual bonding to its text.

At the core of the Qur'anic attachment is the gradual transformation of the

---

[28] For a scholarly treatment on the Qur'an's literary excellence, see Muhammad Abdullah Draz, *The Qur'ān: The Eternal Message* (Leicester, 2001).

reader's temperament and expectations. The Qur'an serves as a vehicle of our inner feelings and aspirations. Our lives are infused with the spirit of the Divine speech which filters in our everyday activities. Matters which are disconnected to the wisdom of Prophethood become inconsequential. Even literature which excels in eloquence pales into insignificance before the majesty of the Qur'an.[29] The Prophetic teachings are timeless and universal and are the fountainhead of all knowledge. There is no pathway to the Qur'an except by embracing its divine message for the eternal guidance of mankind.

Guidelines for Qur'anic Study

Change and continuity in teaching *tafsīr* was a daunting task in the early 20th century in view of the institutional vision of the respective *dār al-'ulūms*. Nadwah[30] was committed to the inclusive knowledge paradigm that transcended the limitation of 'old' and 'new'. In other words, knowledge was a unitary experience based on the universal *iqrā* dimension.

In keeping with this tradition, Shaykh Nadwi developed new approaches to teaching *tafsīr*, keeping in mind the following guidelines:

- Recitation of the Qur'an should establish a personal bond and draw nearness to Allah through it.
- Recitation should be more with contemplation over its meaning and message.
- A working knowledge of Arabic in order to understand the text is essential. Other authentic *tafāsir* should be selectively consulted for this purpose.
- Interaction with the text surpasses the reflection of human thought and knowledge which falls on the clear spring of the Qur'an like the shadow of the tree in clear-crystal water.[31]

Shaykh Nadwi cautions the believers to abstain from negative traits which serve as impediments to appreciating the Qur'an. Pride and a false sense of dignity are drawbacks which stand in the way of following its

---

[29] Nadwi, *Meri Ilm'i wa Mutiila'āti Zindagi* (Rae Bareli, n.d.), 31-2.
[30] On the institutional changes advocated by Nadwah, see, Shams- i-Tabriz Khan, 2 volumes, *Tārikh Nadwat al-'Ulama*, (Lucknow, 1984).
[31] Nadwi, *Studying the Glorious Qur'an: Principles and Methodology* (Leicester, 2003), viii.

teachings. The reformatory changes advocated by the Prophets are met with resistance or defiance and eventually lead to the rejection of Allah's revelations. Likewise, disputation about the Qur'an without proper knowledge enmeshes a person into futile debates. This attitude suggests a hidden pride that builds a hardened outer crust around the heart's receptivity to absorb the divine knowledge and wisdom of the Noble text. Another barrier to profiting from the Qur'an is the denial of the 'Next world' (Hereafter). According to Shaykh Nadwi, the predominance of materialism creates a deficiency in the intellect to accept the realities of the *ākhirah*. There is a tendency among some segments of Muslims to challenge the credibility of revelatory knowledge (*wahy*) based on the distorted interpretation of specific Qur'anic verses which have a clear meaning. A perversion of the mind and withered spiritual outlook are the outcome of rejecting the *ākhirah*. The Qur'an says:

> "Lo! Those who expect not the meeting with Us but desire the life of the world and feel secure therein, and those who are neglectful of our revelations." (10: 7)

According to Shaykh Nadwi, the curriculum designed for Qur'anic studies in general was confined to the conventional teaching of classical commentaries like Jalalayn and Baydawi only. Students were given a general explanation of the Qur'an.

Shaykh Nadwi was appointed lecturer in Arabic literature (*adab*) and *tafsīr* in 1934. His early exposure to Qur'anic studies had begun in his adolescent years which he carried through with sustained fervour at Nadwah. Shaykh Nadwi elaborates:

"During this period, I felt that it was necessary to introduce the Glorious Qur'an to students, to acquaint them with the real purpose and central theme and to prepare and enable them to profit from this Great book. It was also important to warn them about the shortcomings and weaknesses which sometimes prevent one from benefitting fully from the useful effects and blessings which the Qur'an itself has pointed out. These elements comprise the principles and understanding the Glorious Qur'an."[32]

The revisionist approach to *tafsīr* was a specialty of Nadwah. For Shaykh Nadwi Arabic literature blended seamlessly into the profound appreciation

---

[32] Nadwi, *Studying the Glorious Qur'ān: Principles and Methodology* (Leicester, 2003), vii.

of the Qur'an. Too often the *madāris* taught literature in isolation, without recognising its intrinsic importance in the study of the Qur'an. In addition, other disciplines like *hadīth* had to be integrated in order to create an ambience and reverence for the revealed text. In Shaykh Nadwi's estimation, students had to be acquainted with the real purpose and central theme of the Qur'an. These were principles for appreciating and understanding the Book. They serve as a guide and also unravel the timeless significance of the Qur'an.[33]

Shaykh Nadwi's contribution to Qur'anic studies commenced as early as 1934 and was later published as *Studying the Glorious Qur'ān: Principles and Methodology*. The chapters are well-researched and have a direct bearing on contemporary needs.[34] Its lucid style and expressive descriptions are appealing to readers. This book sets to deliver a clear message for the *ummah*: the Qur'anic teachings have relevance for mankind of all times. Shaykh Nadwi says:

> "The Glorious Qur'an is eternal and final from the beginning to the end. It does not contain changing ideals, research or experiments. However, human knowledge may advance. It may broaden the domains of physics, astronomy or prove that the earth is the centre of the universe or that the planets are populated or not–all discoveries would not affect the eternal truths of the glorious Qur'an."[35]

The book is a counterweight to the Orientalists' critique of the Qur'an and also the modernist Muslims' obsession concerning its scientific facts which provide them with leverage to interpret its text arbitrarily and tendentiously. Conventional wisdom dictates that the receptive mind conceives a penetrative soul. Likewise, the key to understanding the Qur'an is a desire for positive change. Preconceived ideas and judgmental tendencies are symptomatic of arrogance and deprivation. The Qur'an diagnoses the malady and offers an effective remedy which promotes the culture of humility for absorbing its message soulfully.[36]

---

[33] Ibid., vii.

[34] For a review of the book by Tabish Mehdi, see Muhsin Usmani, *Mutāla' Tasnifāt i-Sayyid Abul Hasan Ali Nadwi* (Delhi, 2002).

[35] Ibid., *Studying*, 22.

[36] Ibid., 88-90.

Sources of Qur'anic studies

The introductory comments to *Guidance from the Holy Qur'an* brings into focus Shaykh Nadwi's significant contribution to Qur'anic studies.

Although the work is not a complete *tafsīr*, it embodies Shaykh Nadwi's insightful comments on around ninety Qur'anic passages. His elucidation brings into sharper light the eternal guidance of the Qur'an on a wide range of issues relating to both individual and collective life–articles of faith, acts of worship and service to Allah, social relations, morals and manners, laws, religious duties, *sirah*, materialism and lessons from the Qur'an.[37]

Abu Sufyan Islahi succinctly outlines the tenor of Shaykh Nadwi's Qur'anic approach in the light of his speeches and lectures. Two distinctive feature generally marked out his extempore presentation of speeches. First, the verses recited by the Qari at the beginning of the speech was taken up by Shaykh Nadwi to develop his theme. Second, his elucidation of the Qur'anic passages demonstrated the eternal guidance of the sacred text.[38]

Shaykh Nadwi maintained a close association with the Islamic Foundation (Leicester). The aim of his visits was to observe its academic and research programmes as well as its *da'wah* activities. His informal speeches at the premier institution underscored his mastery of *tafsir* and extensive reading of history. In the words of Shaykh Nadwi:

> "However, I have been asked to say a few words. Even as I stand before you my mind is completely blank, but I have entrusted this matter to Allah. It has been my experience that Allah helps in such situations. To be precise, the message of the Qur'an guides me and always provides a way out. The Qur'an being the eternal guidance unravels realities all the time, setting before us numerous dimensions and aspects of its miraculousness.[39]

For Nadwi, Islamic identity is subsumed under the Qur'anic phrase 'complete submission' as an active commitment to uphold its message in totality. Contextual relevance is incorporated in his Qur'anic articulation of

---

[37] Nadwi, *Guidance from the Holy Qur'ān*, xi.

[38] Muhammad Tariq Ayubi, *Mufakkir i-Islam, Sayyid Abul Hasan Ali Nadwi: Apne Afkār ke A'ine me* (Aligarh, 2015).

[39] Nadwi, *Da'wah in the West: The Qur'ānic Paradigm* (Leicester, 1992), 9.

key concepts. In a similar strain, the Qur'an invests mankind with dignity and status that is unprecedented in human history. Its practical application rests with this Qur'anic directive which cuts across racial and linguistic barriers. According to Shaykh Nadwi, communal prejudice and religious bigotry in all forms are a flagrant violation of humanity as enshrined in the Islamic constitution of human rights. Moreover, Shaykh Nadwi expands the Qur'anic notion of equality in the light of circumstantial contexts. In this way the sacred text assumes greater importance in the collective life of Muslims and humanity at large.

CHAPTER 1

Prophetic Methodology: The Qur'anic Paradigm

Function of Prophethood

Shaykh Nadwi reminds the believers that the articles of faith are clearly outlined in the Qur'an. It is therefore not difficult to figure out the Qur'anic worldview on *tawhīd*, for example, because the argument and emphasis are clearly expressed. *Tawhīd* and polytheism (*shirk*) are bipolar terms that separate a believer from a non-believer. A believer who studies the Qur'an seriously can never flounder in his belief in *tawhīd*.[1]

As a Book of eternal guidance, the Qur'an is sent down by Allah so that a believer may derive guidance. It is not an abstract concept that entails complex discussion or debates. By contrast, it is a Book meant for one's reform and self-development "holding out a mirror to one's own shortcomings and as a diagnosis of one's own weaknesses."[2]

Tawhid and guidance, according to Shaykh Nadwi, are the twin pillars of Prophethood. The Prophets serve as a bedrock for delivering Allah's message to the path of salvation. They guide mankind to the ultimate destination (*ākhirah*) by pointing out the way of truth through their preaching (*tabligh*) and divine scriptures.[3]

The overall mission of the Prophets of Allah is examined in Shaykh Nadwi's *Islamic Concept of Prophethood*. The book is based on a series of lectures delivered by him at the University of Madinah in 1962. The thrust of the lectures is embodied in the following extracts:

> "The Holy Prophets (peace be upon them) of Allah are endowed with a unique knowledge which is the fountain of all blessings and salvation. Their knowledge is the light which illuminates the relationship between man and Allah...[the] role of man in the universe and the attitude he should bear towards his Lord. The Prophets (peace be upon them) enlightened us about our good and bad actions and the consequences based on our choice. The knowledge acquired through the Prophets is the knowledge of salvation."

---

[1] Nadwi, *Da'wah in the West: The Qur'ānic Paradigm* (Leicester, 1992), 6-7.

[2] Ibid., 9.

[3] Ibid., 13-14.

"The Prophets are endowed with sound understanding, intellectual talents and refined sensitivity. Keeping themselves away from every other business, they wholeheartedly pursue the course for which they are commissioned by Allah. They always engage themselves with the transmission of divine message on which depends the salvation of man."[4]

According to Shaykh Nadwi, the true concept of Prophethood has been diluted over the last few decades, resulting in the younger generation adopting a somewhat indifferent attitude towards this fundamental aspect of faith. The lecture series had a specific purpose for students studying at university: to highlight the correct understanding about the scope and function of Prophethood.[5]

The way of Prophet Yusuf

In a similar vein, Shaykh Nadwi provides a graphic account on the challenges and opportunities faced by the Prophets. By way of example, the potential to convert adversity into prosperity is recounted in Prophet Yusuf's conversation with his fellow prisoners. The whole episode is characterised by a tactful call to the truth. Prophet Yusuf utilised this everyday situation to deliver the message of *tawhid*. At the same time, he explained the reason for the special knowledge through which he could interpret his follow prisoners' dreams. This special knowledge, Prophet Yusuf emphasized, was not based on family entitlement but rather a reward for renouncing false beliefs. He too, adhered to the faith of his righteous ancestors–a faith of *tawhid* that reflected their total surrender to the will of Allah, His reference to the righteous ancestors, Ibrahim, Ishaq, Yaqub, reaffirms the continuity of *tabligh* by these eminent Prophets.[6]

The Qur'an abounds in narratives on the ebb and flow of previous nations who rejected the teachings of Prophets. Arrogance, disbelief and denial of the Hereafter[7] were the products of their materialistic outlook; hence, their contempt for the Prophets. In these bleak conditions, the Prophets

---

[4] Nadwi, *Islamic Concept of Prophethood* (Lucknow, 1976), 28 (Adapted).

[5] Ibid., 1.

[6] Nadwi, *Guidance fom the Holy Qur'ān*, 263-66.

[7] Surah 11: Hud is representative of the conflict between the power of belief and the forces of disbelief, and transgression of the nations to whom the Prophets were sent to deliver the message of Islam.

persevered in their *tabligh* and placed their reliance on Allah. Success and failure were not the benchmark of their Prophetic call; instead, their call was based on *tawhid*, salvation and reform of society.

Distortion of Prophetic methodology

Shaykh Nadwi draws a distinction between the approach of the Prophets and the contemporary Muslim leaders and activists propagating Islam. In Qur'anic terminology, the call of the Prophets is free from the sophistry of polemics and its mode of expression is forceful and bears the semblance of a life-changing orientation. Thus, the Prophetic appeals reflect the essence and spirit of Islam in its pristine purity. Alluding to the resurgent movements of the twentieth century, Shaykh Nadwi deplores the tendency of those Muslim leaders and political activists who have imported a new vocabulary in their conversation of Islamic revival. Their conceptual framework of revivalism does not always take into account the Prophetic methodology which is derived directly from the Qur'an. In contrast, terms like 'revolution' and 'social order'[8] are invested with an Islamic colouring. Consequently, new meanings and terms of reference are glibly associated (or worse still) attributed to the Qur'an, seemingly in keeping with the spirit of the Book. Not surprisingly, political jargon is unpacked as progressive Islamic thought for the Islamic renewal project. Shaykh Nadwi counsels his audience to take a decisive stand against the misrepresentation of the Qur'an which contains 'distinct truth, intelligible to all ages and circumstances.' The Qur'anic phraseology serves a perennial source of guidance and is intrinsic to our understanding of its content,[9] meaning and teachings. It continues to be understood and interpreted in the light of the following verse:

> "Alif Lam Ra. This is a Divine Command whose contents have been made firm and set forth in detail; (a command) from one Who is All-Wise, All Aware." (11:1)

---

[8] Nadwi, *Islamic Concept of Prophethood*, 40.
[9] Ibid., 55.

Finality of Prophethood

Shaykh Nadwi's insightful comments about the Finality of Prophethood are revealing:

> <<The Qur'an expresses Finality of Prophethood in a unique manner and his universal role after which no divine guidance would be given to man. The phraseology is simple and unambiguous that the religion brought by the last Prophet is perfect, abiding and capable of meeting the needs of human society to the end of time. This day "I have perfected your religion for you and completed my favour upon you and chosen for you Islam as the religion.">> (5: 3)[10]

According to Shaykh Nadwi, there are two distinctive characteristics that define the Finality of Prophethood. First, Islam is "pre-ordained to ascend the pinnacle of glory, to spread its light in the whole world, and to overcome all other religions." This claim is in keeping with the following verse: "He is He Who has sent His Messenger with the guidance and religion of truth that He may cause it to prevail over all religion. And Allah suffices as a witness."[11]
The universality of Prophethood is synonymous with the Holy Prophet's role as the 'Mercy for Mankind'. Therefore, universal values are promoted that transcend the narrow confines of religious bigotry, racial prejudice, social injustice and economic exploitation. For example, universal brotherhood is described as 'a precious gift to mankind'. Nadwi elaborates:

"At the time this declaration (of human rights) was made, mankind was not ready for such a revolutionary concept and thus it was felt as an earthquake and bolt of lightning. However, due to the pioneering efforts of the Islamic states, jurists, scholars and reformers and the advancement which has been made in the past centuries, what was once unthinkable has become commonplace."

For example, the United Nations adopted the Universal Declaration of Human Rights in 1948 and every country and institution of the world makes it an integral part of its constitution.[12]

---

[10] Ibid., 164. Cf. Nadwi, *The Final Prophet and the Perfect Religion* (Lucknow, n.d.).
[11] Ibid., 166.
[12] Nadwi, *Islam, Three Core Beliefs*, 104.

Brotherhood, as explained by Shaykh Nadwi, is interlinked with *khilafah*. Man is elevated as this custodian; therefore, his actions are informed by dignity and respect. He ensures that the resources of the earth are not ravaged by man's greed and exploitative nature. By the same token, the elevated status accorded to man is not reduced to a rubble of humiliation and perpetual suffering.[13] According to Nadwi, human rights have been trampled in the past centuries which is in sharp contrast to the unequivocal declaration by the Qur'an.

Just imagine how dreadful society would be when man considers his fellow human beings as subhuman. In the past thousands of lives used to be sacrificed for the pleasure of a single individual. There were rulers who devastated country after country. Alexander (356–323BC) came from Macedonia up to India and destroyed many nations and civilisations on the way. Julius Caesar (100-44BC) killed people savagely. More recently, millions of people lost their lives in the two World Wars of the twentieth century. All of this happened due to ego, arrogance, greed for power and the control of the economy.[14]

In sum, Shaykh Nadwi contextualises the gamut of human activity under the ambit of Finality of Prophethood. As such the Qur'anic declaration is unambiguous: Islam is the culmination of the previous revealed religions and is perfect for mankind. For the *ummah*, in particular, it manifests itself in the shari'ah which is a divine code of guidance. There is no alteration in the basic principles of Islam which are steadfastly observed across the world irrespective of different time zones and climatic conditions. Essentially, variation does not conflict with universality and this for example is best expressed in the five obligatory prayers.

In blatant opposition to Muslim sensibilities, the nineteenth century claimant to Prophethood, Mirza Ghulam Ahmad Qadiani (d. 1908) represented a conspiracy and a clandestine revolt against the universal declaration of the Qur'an in respect of the finality of Prophethood.

A shared characteristic of the deviant movements like Qadianism is their avowed aim to dismantle the Finality of Prophethood creed and impose the supposed divine status of their founders on the masses. Therefore, it is hardly surprising when they develop a parallel system of beliefs and practices to Islam. No doubt, the element of charisma is given credence to bolster their religious profile. At the same time, new–fangled and multi–hued interpretations are conceived to vindicate their dubious claims to

---

[13] Ibid., 107.
[14] Ibid., 108. Cf. Nadwi, *Qur'āni Ifāda,* vol. 2 (Rae Bareli, 2013), 254 -7.

Prophethood.

Mirza Ahmad Qadiani adopted a polemical style in his writings that had the hallmark of 'self–advertisement and self-glorification'.[15] The central theme of his *Barāhin i- Ahmadiya* is the continuity of divine revelation. His flashes of inspiration are captured in his incoherent collection of Qur'anic verses interspersed with a bizarre assortment of poetry.[16] In reality, his notorious penchant for ascribing divine sanction to mundane matters is suggestive of his personality disorder.

Shaykh Nadwi makes an incisive assessment about the audacious claims of the Mirza in respect of Prophethood:

The claim of divine communication (*wahy*) is in fact a hidden conspiracy, a clandestine revolt against Prophethood as well. If this process were to be considered a widespread and unceasing activity, Prophets would no longer remain necessary at all. The Qur'an and other scriptures link true guidance, knowledge of God, His attributes, of His Will and all the matters relating to the unseen world with prophethood... In fact, if these concepts (Qadiani beliefs) were to be taken seriously then religious faith would become something akin to the spiritual feats such as occultism (and other deviant trends) which are becoming popular in the present times.[17]

According to Shaykh Nadwi, it is a disingenuous attempt to distort the Qur'anic terminology for political or religious expediency. In his reading of Islamic history Shaykh Nadwi points out to deviants sects like the Batinites[18] who interpolated esoteric meanings into the unambiguous Qur'anic text. Their avowed aim was to dislodge the concept of Prophethood and to create new boundaries for their pseudo-rational interpretation of the Qur'an. Notwithstanding the grave dangers posed by heretical movements, Iqbal (d. 1938), the poet of the East, who was a man of rare insight and had also studied the Qadiani movement made the following observation:

"The life-history of nations shows that when the tide of a people begins to ebb, decadence itself becomes a source of inspiration; inspiring poets, philosophers, saints and statesmen are turned into

---

[15] Nadwi, *Qadianism A Critical Study* (Lucknow, 1974), 30.

[16] Ibid., 31-2.

[17] Ibid., 133-134.

[18] On the Batinite heresy, see Nadwi, *Saviours of Islamic Spirit*, vol.1, 108-12. This movement adopted some aspects of Greek philosophy –an accretion of doctrinal beliefs which were condemned by Sunni scholar.

a class of apostles whose sole ministry is to glorify, by the force of a seductive art or logic, all that is ignoble and ugly in the life of their people. These apostles unconsciously clothe despair in the glaring garments of hope, undermine the traditional values of conduct and thus destroy the spiritual virility of those who happen to be their victims."[19]

Da'wah: An Overview

Shaykh Nadwi's literary output is characterised by his wide reading of history, comparative religious studies and biographical literature. According to the celebrated figure of Islamic revivalist movements, Shaykh Yusuf Qardāwī , the Nadwah vision of traditional Islamic disciplines integrated with modern knowledge was best represented in Shaykh Nadwi's multifaceted career.

It was the *imāni* factor[20] that delineated his notable contributions to the various fields of Islamic learning. This impression is shared by Muhammad Mustafa Bahjat who says that Shaykh Nadwi can be compared to prominent Islamic figures like Ibn Taymiyyah, and Ibn Abd-al Barr (d. 1463); their writings on Qur'anic studies, *hadīth* and *sirah* were wide-ranging and influential. Shaykh Nadwi's early education provided him with this versatility "[to] enter into the different fields of Islamic and social sciences through a wide door".[21]

The *imāni* factor accounted for Shaykh Nadwi's ability to deliver a lecture extempore based on the recitation of specific verses in conferences and seminars.

The central concept of the Qur'an's eternal guidance in the light of the Prophets' lives is elaborated in Shaykh Nadwi's formulation of *da'wah*. Terms like *tabligh* and teachings are therefore, interchangeably used in this volume. Departing from the conventional understanding of *da'wah*, Shaykh Nadwi expands its boundaries to develop the Qur'anic perspective on its all-encompassing influence.

---

[19] Muhammad Iqbal, *Islam and Ahmadism*, (Lucknow, 1974), 17.
[20] Nadwi, *Da'wah in the West: The Qur'ānic Paradigm*, 9.
[21] Cited in Mohammad Akram Nadwi, *Shaykh Abul Hasan Ali Nadwi: His Life and Works* (Batley, 2013), 53.

Salient features of *da'wah*

We now refer to three aspects or more appropriately dimensions of *da'wah* that serve as the perennial source of guidance for the *ummah*. According to Shaykh Nadwi, *da'wah* and guidance have priority (*awwaliyah*) over the commands and shari'ah in the Qur'an. It is because the foundation of faith (*imān*) is guidance (*hidāyah*) and 'to believe' depends on *da'wah* which is paraphrased as an invitation to Allah.[22] The following verse is a telling example of *da'wah*:

> "Invite (the people) to the way of your Lord with wisdom and fair exhortation..." (16: 125)

It is a living miracle of the Qur'an that it has not set any limits to *da'wah*. However, it has left it to the discretion and better judgement of the one who invites. He has to consider the requirements of *da'wah* which are outlined in the above verse.

The *way of your Lord* (*sabil*), as explained by Shaykh Nadwi, opens new horizons of thought and action. It covers every aspect of human activity related to the call (or invitation) and the methods are adopted according to needs and circumstantial settings. It is, therefore, not binding that *da'wah* be made only through the spoken word, writing or public talk. Effective methods that are permissible according to shari'ah may be adopted.[23]

Two constituents make up the character of *da'wah*: wisdom (*hikmah*) and exhortation (*maw'izah*). These key terms are not easy to translate in any other language as they convey profound and comprehensive meanings. Shaykh Nadwi draws our attention to the single expression (*hikmah*) and its connotations which are not limited to semantic analysis. He observes:

> "In keeping with the level of understanding, capacity, social customs, regional variations, taste, interests, contemporary issues and challenges and psychological factors and more importantly, the belief and worldview of the persons at whom *da'wah* is directed, one should evolve suitable norms. Every mode of expression for winning over the addressee should be included in this."[24]

---

[22] Nadwi, *Inviting to the Way of Allah* (London, 1996), 8-9.

[23] Ibid., 11.

[24] Nadwi, *Guidance from the Holy Qur'ān*, 19. 'Abdullah 'Abbas Nadwi reinforces Shaykh Nadwi's view in his *Mir Kārwān* (New Delhi, 1999), 122.

In detailing the *da'wah* factor of certain Prophets based on the Qur'anic accounts, Shaykh Nadwi states categorically that truth is the hallmark of their methodology. Likewise, he cautions against blatant self-interest like political motives or polemical sophistry. Muslims are required to draw valuable lessons from the stories of the Prophets. By the same token, the Prophetic model of *da'wah* should be emulated which has specified the role of the Muslim community. They have a particular mission to implement as outlined in the following verse:

> "You (true believers in Islam) are the best of peoples ever raised up
> for mankind. You enjoin good, forbid evil and believe in Allah"
>
> (3: 110)

According to Shaykh Nadwi, there is no parochial status assigned to the Muslim community. Mankind, as we observe, is on the verge of collapse and ruin. It is only the Muslim community tasked with this onerous responsibility of enjoining good and forbidding evil that can facilitate the moral regeneration of the ailing humanity.[25] Shaykh Nadwi refers to the famous incident drawn from the pages of Islamic history which echoes the universal dimension of *da'wah*:

> <<Rabi' bin 'Amir was scheduled to deliver the message of Islam to the commander-in-chief, Rustom, of the Persian empire. Emboldened by his faith and confidence in the universality of Islam, his forceful words are of relevance to *da'wah* workers:
> "Allah sent us so that we may liberate our fellow human beings from subservience to fellow human beings and bring them to obedience to One True God. We are here to take them from the narrowness of the world to its spaciousness. Our aim is to free them of the persecution perpetrated against them by other religions. We want to bless them with the justice and equity of Islam.">>[26]

Rabi's immortal address to Rustom is inseparably linked to the concept of

---

[25] Ibid., 36-39.
[26] Nadwi, *The Role and Responsibilities of Muslims in the West.* Translated by Abdur Raheem Kidwai (Leicester, 1993), 16-17. Cf. Nadwi, *Islam and The World*, 59.

justice (*'adl*) in Islam. After the termination of Prophethood it was the *Sahābah* who shouldered the responsibility of *da'wah*. They had no political ambitions; instead, their unwavering focus was to recast the mould of humanity on the guidelines provided in the Qur'an and the exemplary Prophetic conduct. According to Shaykh Nadwi, the Qur'anic influence in charting a new course for humanity is pervasive:

> "The world obtained a fresh lease of life; justice and fairness became its hallmark; the weak were liberated from the haughty and the mighty, mercy and kindness became norms. It was the time when altruism became a driving force, faith and conviction captured human hearts, mankind began to take pride in selflessness, and virtuous behaviour became habitual with people."[27]

Shaykh Nadwi's embodiment of the *da'wah* ideals

It may be noted that Shaykh Nadwi's *da'wah* presentation is based on its universal trajectory which offers hope to humanity bedevilled by moral decline. Shaykh Nadwi's personal profile helps us to understand his unique position among his contemporaries in respect of his *da'wah* methodology for Muslim individuals, professionals and organisations.

Let us turn to Muhammad Marah's description of Shaykh Nadwi's *da'wah* qualities.

Balanced Disposition

Following the Qur'anic directive of *wasatiyyah*[28], Shaykh Nadwi's methodology[29] is informed by a balanced approach to the divergent expression of *tablighi* activities. In other words, extremism (*tashaddud*) which over the last few decades has become a salience of several Islamic movements portraying the *salaf* tradition, is considered a bane by Shaykh Nadwi. Clearly, Shaykh Nadwi is categorical in his presentation of *tawhid* against the accretion of *shirk*-laden rituals adopted by certain segments of the Muslim community. *Tawhīd*, Shaykh Nadwi argues, is non-

---

[27] Nadwi, *Mankind's Debt to the Prophet Muhammad* (Oxford, 1992), 11.

[28] For a detailed discussion on *wasatiyyah*, see Jakob Skovgaard- Peterson and Bettina Graff (ed.), *Global Mufti: The Phenomenon of Yusuf al-Qardāwi* (London, 2009), 213-28.

[29] See Tariq Ayubi (ed.), *Proceedings of the International Conference on Contemporary Thought and Vision of Shaykh Abul Hasan Ali Nadwi* (Aligarh, 2015), 53.

negotiable; it is a leitmotif in the Qur'anic declaration about the order of the universe and the Prophets strove relentlessly to propagate it to all nations.[30]

In the political sphere, Shaykh Nadwi maintained a balanced approach towards Islamic organisations and movements clamouring for an Islamic state. The tone of *wasatiyyah* is based on moderation or harmony and equilibrium (*i'tidāl*) which is not swayed by excess (*ghulu*) or laxity (*tafrit*). According to Shaykh Nadwi, a conciliatory approach does not suggest signs of inferiority complex or a surrender to the West but reflects a pragmatism that characterises the vision of *da'wah* as shown by the Holy Prophet (peace be upon him). Thus, the reconstruction of society is a prerequisite to develop a viable model for an Islamic state.

The balanced approach to *da'wah* adopted by Shaykh Nadwi was not confined to Muslim countries; in fact, he invoked the Qur'anic text to address the Muslim communities who constitute minorities in the West. His visionary interaction with Muslim minorities is discussed elsewhere in the study.

Two points emerge from our discussion of Shaykh Nadwi's balanced disposition. First, the term *wasatiyyah* is distinguishable from moderate Islam, which is a pacified surrender to the political agenda advanced by Muslim regimes. Second, a distinction must be made between *salaf* and *salaiyyah*. The latter has morphed into an anti-*turāth* (legacy) movement with self-certified credentials of representing a purist version of Islam.

Comprehensive Study

Shaykh Nadwi placed emphasis on the Qur'an and sunnah as nodal points to amplify a broader understanding of *da'wah*. His audience varied in their intellectual capacity and orientation. Across the spectrum of divergent opinions, Shaykh Nadwi's scholarly temperament touched the hearts of Muslims committed to Islamic resurgence. His winning formula was his in-depth study of an array of subjects and his absolute faith in propagating the faith and practice of Islam. Significantly, Shaykh Nadwi did not disconnect from the 'ulama and *mashā'ikh* in whose lives he saw the Qur'anic model of *da'wah*.[31] They were the true representatives of the Islamic ideal and a

---

[30] Muhammad Marah, "Al-Hikmah was Khasa'isuha al-Khitab al Da'iyyah li al-Shaykh Abul Hasan Ali Nadwi", in Tariq Aubi Nadwi (ed.). *Proceedings of the International Conference Shaykh Abul Hasan Ali Nadwi* (Aligarh 2015), 53.
[31] Marah, *Al-Hikmah*, 56-7.

collective voice of *islāh* (reform) and *tajdīd* (renewal).[32] Shaykh Nadwi maintained that a strong Muslim community served as a buffer zone against the incursion of alien systems that sought to undermine its *tabligh* purpose of enjoining what is good and forbidding what is evil. To this end, he envisaged a strong leadership that could steer the destiny of the Muslim *ummah*.

Brevity of expression

As a litterateur, Shaykh Nadwi employed the best mode of expression to communicate the dimensions of *da'wah*. Archaic prose or dogmatic expression generally vitiates the power of elegance in speeches or lectures. Likewise, translations of the Qur'an that teem with jargon and unidiomatic expressions have a negative impact on the readers' close association with and appreciation of the divine text. In this regard, Shaykh Nadwi avoids the trodden path of mediocrity. His *da'wah* lectures and writings are infused with persuasive expressions gleaned from the Qur'an, *hadīth* literature and literary genres of accomplished scholars over the centuries. Consider the *ismi'i* and *tuhfah* genres[33] which were addressed to the Arab and subcontinental Muslims respectively. They are informed by a poignancy that is unmistakably *imāni* in content and drawn from the Qur'anic verses dealing with *da'wah*, accountability and *islāh*.[34]

The term *ismi'i* is used as a rhetorical device by Shaykh Nadwi to address the Arab world about its commitment to Islam as a complete way of life. It is also an impassioned appeal to Arab Muslims to embrace Islamic culture and civilisation wholeheartedly. The *tuhfah* writing addresses Muslims in the subcontinent. It is a 'gift' that explores themes of Muslim self-identity, dialogue with other faith groups and most importantly, the reconstruction of Muslim society. Muhammad Majzub, a noted scholar of Arabic literature, shares a similar sentiment:

"A person who closely examines the writings of Shaykh Nadwi will perceive that its literary expressions have a certain enchantment which is only found among the notable personalities

---

[32] For a detailed analysis of these terms, see Abdul Kader Choughley. *Islamic Resurgence: Sayyid Abul Hasan Ali Nadwi and his Contemporaries* (New Delhi; 2011), 4-95.
[33] The thematic significance of the *ismi'i* and *tuhfah* series is examined in Abdul Kader Choughley, *Sayyid Abul Hasan Ali Nadwi: Life and Works* (New Delhi, 2012), 172-6.
[34] Marah, *Al-Hikmah*, 57.

who have a deep knowledge of the intricacies of words, who have interacted with them, and whose hearts have been most affected by what they were composing. This is the primary trait which people of spiritual taste possessed from among those who have studied the Qur'an."[35]

Likewise, Shaykh Nadwi lucidly describes the power of the Holy Prophet's (peace be upon him) words which are inextricably linked to the inimitable language of the Qur'an:

"What can you say of a human being whose tongue was softened by the Qur'an, in whose flesh the blood of the Qur'an became interfused. [It] flowed in him as the spirit flows in the body, whose essence captivated and overwhelmed his heart. Indeed, the Qur'an was poured into his heart and took control over him in a manner that is known only to Allah."[36]

Qardāwī wrote a personal account about the life and times of Shaykh Nadwi.[37] He delineated the outstanding qualities of Shaykh Nadwi as a *dā'i*. Two qualities in particular made him an unrivalled scholar among his peers and contemporaries:

Shaykh Nadwi was *Qur'āni* because the Book of Allah was his main source of inspiration and his constant companion both inwardly and outwardly. He recited, studied, taught and lived by it. He strove throughout his life to be an embodiment of the Qur'anic teachings.

Also Shaykh Nadwi was a *Rabbāni*, a word uniquely associated with the rich Arabic language. He possessed an aura of holiness and the highest levels of spiritual perfection in which practice fused with moral excellence (*ihsān*).[38] He (Shaykh Nadwi) thus lived among the latter generation (*khalaf*) but led a life of the former generation (*salaf*).[39]

Shaykh Nadwi's detachment form worldly pursuits and focus on emulating the lives of the earliest representatives of Islam (*salaf*) is reaffirmed by Qardāwī.

---

[35] Akram, *Shaykh Abul Hasan*, 90.
[36] Ibid., 91.
[37] Yusuf Qardawi, *Shaykh Abul Hasan Ali Nadwi, Kamā 'Araftāh* (Damascus, 2001).
[38] Ibid., 10-12 (paraphrased).
[39] Akram Nadwi, *Shaykh Abul Hasan*, 170.

Payām i-Insāniyat: Global *Da'wah*

In his formulation of *da'wah*, Shaykh Nadwi saw no contradiction in presenting the Qur'anic message of peace and harmony to non-Muslims in the country.

In the aftermath of the partition in 1947, Shaykh Nadwi saw the reconstruction of society as integral to a stable and progressive India. His speeches[40] beginning from the 1950s touched on vital issues affecting the nation. Over a relatively short period of time the initiatives undertaken to bring closer the various communities in a multireligious and plural society yielded positive results. In fact, a series of speeches were warmly received by both intellectuals and lay persons and eventually became the forerunner to the establishment of *Payām i-Insāniyat* (Message for Humanity). It would be worthwhile to examine the thematic significance (as well as the appropriate measures) contained in these speeches in order to appreciate the thrust of Shaykh Nadwi's presentation of a new social order. The following points deserve special mention:

- An incorrigible growth of anarchy.
- Widespread corruption the proliferation of selfish interest and disintegration of moral values.[41]

As a remedy to the above malaise, Shaykh Nadwi maintains that society should reassess its role as an agent of change. This can only be possible if the starting point to initiate changes is linked to the heart which is the repository of moral values. Unless moral regeneration is fully implemented, no society will be free from these vices which mirror a peculiar form of *Jāhiliyyah* (Ignorance). Moreover, it was also the temperament of the Prophets to remove vices of the heart in order to reconstruct an ideal society.

Shaykh Nadwi used the forum of the *Payām* (established in 1974) to advocate better relations between Muslims and members of other faith groups.[42] The inspiration, according to Shaykh Nadwi, was the Qur'anic dictum exhorting Muslims to 'enjoin what is good and forbid what is evil.' The Qur'anic

---

[40] Nadwi, *Payām i-Insāniyat* (Lucknow, 2004) is a collection of speeches delivered in 1954 which touched primarily on the role of the Prophets in creating a revolutionary environment for the betterment of humanity.

[41] Muhammad Rabey Nadwi, *Sayyid Abul Hasan Ali Nadwi: An Eminent Scholar, Thinker and Reformer.* (New Delhi, 2014), 141-2.

[42] Nadwi, *Karwān*, vol. 2, 119-23.

declaration served as an impetus for the Muslim community to join hands with members of other faiths in the country. Shaykh Nadwi began addressing joint Hindu-Muslim public rallies, calling for communal harmony and peace. His speeches generally focused on moral values, communal hatred, violence and oppression of marginalised groups, social vices and corruption in public life which destroyed the fabric of a stable Indian society.[43]

According to Shaykh Nadwi, the essence of the *Payām* was to exemplify the teachings of Islam through Muslim interaction with others. Not only was this their religious duty, it was also indispensable if they were to live in security and peace as a minority group.

In presenting the teachings of Islam to a mixed audience, Shaykh Nadwi tactfully referred to specific teachings of the Prophets which had resonance for the Indian society in general. Likewise, reference was made to the lives of the *Sahābah*, highlighting their spirit of self-sacrifice and mutual love. These telling examples are illustrative of Shaykh Nadwi's vision of interweaving the teachings of Islam into the fabric of the Indian society.[44]

The need for divine guidance is articulated by Shaykh Nadwi:

> "The Messengers of Allah placed restraint on desires and urged man to be moderate in gratifying his desires. Far from stoking base desires they infused into man a strong desire for pleasing Allah and developing sympathy for mankind.
>
> We are keen on instilling the above quest for truth. Life does not stand for eating or drinking. Man should not lead a materialistic or animal life. We wish to infuse a new thirst which may sound novel today. However, our message is the one which was brought by all Messengers to their respective communities. The same message was most forcefully and clearly presented by Holy Prophet Muhammad (peace be upon him) as the final word. The truth should be reiterated everywhere."[45]

It may be noted that the *Payām* was not an extension of the *tabligh* movement nor did it envisage a syncretic unity of religions (*wahdat-i-adyān*)[46]. In this context, the subcontinent in the past had experienced a

---

[43] Rabey Nadwi, *An Eminent Scholar*, 147-8.
[44] See Nadwi, *Towards Salvaging Humanity* (Springs, 2019).
[45] Ibid., 14-5.
[46] Shaykh Nadwi invoked the Qur'anic dictum of 'enjoining what is good, and

syncretic faith which aimed to dismantle Islam as a universal religion. On the contrary, in his public speeches, Shaykh Nadwi made reference to the sailing ship analogy employed by the Holy Prophet (peace be upon him) to highlight the destiny of both Muslims and other faith groups.

The following *hadīth* in *Bukhāri* and *Tirmidhi* alludes to this:

> "It has been reported by Nu'mān ibn Bashir that the Holy Prophet (peace be upon him) said: "There are two people who do not transgress the limits of Allah, and there are others who do so. They are like two groups who boarded a ship; one of them settled on the upper deck, and the other, on the lower deck. So, when the people of the lower deck needed water, they said: 'Why should we cause trouble to the people of the upper deck when we can easily have plenty of water by making a hole in our deck? 'Now, if the people of the upper deck do not prevent this group from such foolishness, all of them will perish.""

In the final analysis, Shaykh Nadwi highlights the powerful influence of love in its real sense. It is not a philosophical abstraction or a spiritual construct; its dynamism and vitality continue to shape the lives of humanity. Shaykh Nadwi says:

> "The excellence of man lies in his love and mercy for others: one person is pricked with a thorn but another person feels the pain. Man is gifted with tears which fall from his eyes when he sees a widow's head uncovered in helplessness, a poor man's kitchen unlit and a sick man in distress. The quality of love permeating through the human heart is a very precious gift of Allah. When something stirs it, it assumes a strange power. It rises above the considerations of religion, community, nation and motherland. It then only sees another man's heart and feels its suffering and is drawn to it as naturally as an iron chip is pulled towards a magnet."[47]

In his pursuit of a new social order for both Muslims and Hindus, Shaykh

---

forbidding what is evil' to reassure wary 'ulama and other concerned groups that the Islamic character of the *Payām* was not compromised.

[47] Nadwi, *Islam and Introduction* (Lucknow, 1998), 152. Cf. Nadwi, *Towards Salvaging Humanity.*

Nadwi could not escape the scathing criticism of dissenting Muslim voices. Their motive was clear: no co-existence was possible with the significant 'Other'. However, Shaykh Nadwi remained steadfast in   his resolve, and undeterred by these hostile comments, pursued a course that he believed would foster better relations between Muslims and other faith groups.

The activities of the *Payām* were twofold: First, the communities in India could progress only in a climate of peace, free from inter-communal violence. Second, bringing Muslims and others to work together, Shaykh Nadwi believed, would provide a means for the Muslims to carry out their responsibilities of *tabligh* in a constructive way.

The *Payām* had a considerable impact on changing the mindset of many citizens belonging to different faiths in the country. It fervently believed in the unity of mankind which effectively had the potential to bring about lasting peace not only in India but across the world. In Shaykh Nadwi's estimation the malaise affecting mankind was a global phenomenon. Therefore, the remedy derived from divine sources was clear and consistent.

Da'wah in The West: The Qur'anic Approach

Shaykh Nadwi's travels to Europe and US during the period 1963–96[48] broadened his intellectual horizon and gave him an in-depth understanding of the conflictual relationship between Islam and the West. Even in his critique of the West, he saw opportunities for a sustained Muslim presence in Europe, particularly Britain, which owing to its colonial past now was a major role player in its interaction with Muslim immigrants drawn from South Asia.

The establishment of the Oxford Centre of Islamic Studies (OCIS)[49] in 1985 of which he was the Chairman was aimed at creating a forum for a better understanding of Islam in the West. As early as in 1983 Shaykh Nadwi was invited to read a paper on *Islam and the West*[50] at the inaugural ceremony of

---

[48] Refer to the following books on Shaykh Nadwi's *da'wah* travels to Europe and United States:

- *Speaking Plainly to the West* (Lucknow, 1976).
- *Muslims in the West: The Message and Mission.* Edited by Khurram Murad (Leicester, 1983).

[49] On the establishment of OCIS. See Nadwi, *Karwan.* vol. 2, 374-81.

[50] Nadwi, *Islam and the West* (Lucknow, 1983).

OCIS Centre. He welcomed its establishment as an event of significance not only for the West but for the world as a whole. He noted:

> "[It] is the symbol of a healthy development in human relationships and should contribute towards a happy future for mankind – a future in which the misgivings of the past will disappear, and the evil shadow of distorted history will fade. The Centre will, I hope, embark on search for truth and the acquisition of knowledge which will lay the basis for co-operation and harmony between different people."[51]

As the chairman of the Centre, Shaykh Nadwi was influential in creating a better understanding of Islam in the West.

The Qur'anic message and the impact of the Prophetic teachings saw the publication of the following lecture of Shaykh Nadwi by the Centre, titled *Islam and Knowledge*.[52] Shaykh Nadwi developed the theme of the *iqrii* paradigm in which the eternal values of revealed guidance can inform analytical interpretations in modern scholarship. Another monograph *Mankind's Debt to the Prophet Muhammad (peace be upon him)*[53] discusses, albeit briefly, the life and teachings of the Holy Prophet (peace be upon him). The precious gifts which are outlined by Shaykh Nadwi in the lecture are gleaned from the universal teachings of the Qur'an. The contributions of Islam include the following:

- The clear and unambiguous creed of *tawhid.*
- The concept of human equality and brotherhood.
- Integration of knowledge and religion.
- The establishment of a universal creed and culture.[54]

Likewise, Shaykh Nadwi supported the establishment of Islamic institutions with a non-sectarian bias, which produced Islamic literature reflecting a strong *da'wah* element. A premier institute with a strong publishing network, the Islamic Foundation (Leicester) has played a

---

[51] OCIS News: Special Issue (2000), 2.

[52] Nadwi, *Islam and Knowledge* (Oxford, 1988).

[53] Nadwi, *Mankind's Debt to the Prophet Muhammad (peace be upon him)*, (Oxford, 1989).

[54] Nadwi, *Islam and Civilisation* (Lucknow, 1986).

significant role in disseminating the multifaceted aspects of Islam in the West.

Its publishing output has been admirable, and it has over the years complemented its interfaith dialogues and seminars to promote a better understanding of Islam in Europe. Although the Foundation has a strong Jamā'at i-Islami affiliation, Shaykh Nadwi maintained a cordial relationship with its core leadership. His regular visits and lectures, some of which were published by the Foundation, demonstrated a mutual respect and affection. His analytical writings on the West and Muslim responsibility in communicating the message of Islam reflect his shared interest and concerns with the Foundation in this important field. Several of Shaykh Nadwi's writings focusing on Muslim interaction with the West were published by the institute.[55] In one of his published lectures Shaykh Nadwi relates the following Qur'anic simile to *da'wah*:

> "Do you not see how Allah sets forth a parable? A goodly word is as a goodly tree, whose root is firmly fixed and its branches reach the sky, giving it fruits all times, by the leave of its Lord. Allah sets forth parables for mankind in order that they may remember." (14: 24-25)

According to Shaykh Nadwi, the above verses provide a graphic account "of how to carry out *da'wah* in any given time and place: how to introduce Islam, how to invite people to it; how to highlight distinctive features; and how to guide man in both this life and the next."

In the light of the simile employed the following points are linked to the Qur'anic vision of *da'wah*. Linguistic competence (*kalimatun tayyibah*) and sincerity are effective communicators of *da'wah*. It should be illumined by an inner light and conveyed with heartfelt conviction in order to bring about real changes in the hearts and minds of the audience. Therefore, these distinctive features should be emphasized while keeping in mind the intellectual temperament of non-Muslims in the West.

This approach has been explained by Qardāwī:

> "[Shaykh Nadwi] had a profound understanding of the gulf that existed between Western and Islamic civilisation, in particular the educational, cultural and moral crisis that set them apart ... [He] adopted the third approach which was neither a blind imitation (of the West) nor remained insulated from the benefits that it offered in

---

[55] For example, Nadwi, *Islam and the West.*

terms of science and technology. Thus, he steered away from a polemical approach towards the West and adopted a course that would serve as a sign post for both civilisation."[56]

The above approach is reiterated by Shaykh Nadwi: All of us should be prompted only by the ideal of seeking the pleasure of Allah and preaching the message of Islam in its pristine form to others. Allah will guide them and those who directed them to the message of Islam and provided them with materials. They will be rewarded by Allah. There should not, however, be any sectarian interest or personality cult in our approach. We must present Islam in its totality and as the message of the truth. Islam is not anyone's monopoly. Our message in this Christian environment and Western setting should be the one which the Qur'an puts thus:

"Come to a common word between us and you; that we shall serve none but Allah and shall associate none with Him in His divinity and that some of us will not take others as lords besides Allah." (3:64)[57]

Shaykh Nadwi expresses his candour about the proliferation of cult worship in relation to *tasawwuf*. A more concerning trend is the inflated superior status attributed to the *mashā'ikh* by their respective followers. A closer reading of the Qur'an blurs out the distinction of superiority, regardless of religiosity or nobility of family pedigree.

Da'wah for the Western Audience

The following summation and analysis of Shaykh Nadwi's thinking is based largely on his work, *Muslims in the West*. Shaykh Nadwi is unequivocal with regard to the ultimate goals of *da'wah*, which he seeks to further. For him, *da'wah* implies that Muslim presence in the West can have only one justification: to reach out to non-Muslims both by word and example. A Muslim cannot exist as a Muslim unless he fulfils the mission entrusted to him by Allah and His Holy Prophet (peace be upon him).

Shaykh Nadwi's *da'wah* vision is rooted in the noble example of the Prophet Muhammad (peace be upon him).

---

[56] Qardāwī, "Mufakkir Hadhrat Mawlana Abul Hasan Ali Nadwi ki Rahnuma Da'wah i-Usul", in *Fikr i-Islami* (Basti, 2000-1), 207-19.
[57] Nadwi, *Da'wah in the West: The Qur'ānic Paradigm* (Leicester, 1992), 19.

Prophetic Mission

Shaykh Nadwi reiterates his view that the Prophetic mission should serve as the reference point for a meaningful understanding of *da'wah*. All the Prophets that came and the last of the Prophets, Muhammad (peace be upon him), had the 'making of a new man' as their sole concern. They opened to man the infinite forces within. They awakened in him his hidden possibilities. They opened the eye of the heart that he could see the Creator of this great universe and receive the treasures of guidance. Citing the following verse: *The Lord of East and West; there is no God save Him; so you should choose Him alone for your guidance* (73: 9), Shaykh Nadwi maintains that the Prophets liberated man from all forms of idolatry and dualism, from superstition and subservience to irrational tradition and from every submission except submission to the Creator of the universe.

Prophetic Methodology

Rooted in divine guidance, the Prophetic methodology, Shaykh Nadwi contends, did not touch on mundane matters but sought to put before man the "right kind of objectives, to draw from the highest desire, the highest commitment." Addressing the Western world, Shaykh Nadwi makes an impassioned appeal for them to turn to the Prophetic revelation exemplified by Islam for salvation.

What does Islam offer to the Western mind? His response is twofold: the Qur'anic teachings with their inexhaustible intellectual wealth, which can still put new life into the nations of the world, are capable of facing the problems of modern times. Prophet Muhammad's (peace be upon him) life and the wisdom of his teachings are applicable to all, covering a wide variety of situations and problems.

However, Shaykh Nadwi states that for the Western nations to turn to Islam requires moral courage and admission of failure. This is not possible, Shaykh Nadwi argues for the following reasons:

"Those man in power in the West would rather see nations destroyed, landscapes and resources devastated, the whole of humanity plunged into distress, than make the admission. A false sense of prestige and inflated pride in their scientific and material progress, prevents them from turning to the life of that unlettered Holy Prophet (peace be upon him) who alone offers the hope of salvation. The result of this self-conceit is that generations of mankind face destruction."

Against this gloomy background, Shaykh Nadwi offers hope to mankind by expressing the need for world leadership to access its spiritual resources from the message of the Holy Prophet (peace be upon him) which will 'lead humanity to its rightful destiny'. Shaykh Nadwi boldly states that such a step would require a revolution, a tremendous capacity for sacrifice, to move from one way of life to another–in short, a profound revolution that would make leaders the example of humanity[58]. This clarion call, he insists, is explained by the following verse:

"We wished to be gracious to those who were being depressed in the land, to make them leaders (in faith) and make them heirs." (28: 5)

For Shaykh Nadwi, if the West wished to discover the secret to the world and guide humanity by it, it would not do so. The West can unlock its potential and capabilities through its technological advancement. It can nurture its scientific progress; however, it is deprived of that spiritual outlook. Shaykh Nadwi reminds the West that the only key is faith (*imān*), "[that] key was gifted to humanity by the Prophets, which has been lost, or is buried beneath the dreary weight of modern civilisation or under the ruins of houses of worship."[59]

Shaykh Nadwi's critique is characterised by his acknowledgement of the West's strides in science and technology. However, he adds a cautionary note regarding the alarming trends in Muslim countries that have either surrendered to the West or have insulated themselves from its positive features.[60] The consequences of such conflicting attitude are glaring: Muslim subservience which has stripped away its own collective Islamic identity or its resistance to appropriating in a meaningful way the benefits of science and technology offered by the West has created irredeemable void in Muslim countries.

In a similar vein, he reminds the West of its obligation to subordinate its phenomenal achievement within a religious moral and spiritual framework:[61]

---

[58] Nadwi, *Muslims in the West: The Message and Mission* (Leicester, 1983).

[59] Ibid., 36.

[60] Ibid.,70.

[61] For a critique on Muslim attitude towards Western civilisation, see Nadwi, *Western*

"We do not grudge you your attainments. We do not regard your progress with contempt. What we do ask you most earnestly is [to] subordinate your worldly possessions and phenomenal achievements to the Will of God. Place it all under the control and authority of the Divine law. Use it for the rebirth and rescue of mankind; for the generation of an atmosphere of universal (non-exclusive) equality and fraternity and justice and freedom from fear in the world."[62]

Qur'anic Concept of *Khilafah*

To bring home this moral responsibility more clearly, Shaykh Nadwi refers to the following Qur'anic concept of *khilāfah*.

"I am about to place a vicegerent in the earth..."(2: 30)

Islam places the crown of custodianship on man's head, and there can be no greater honour. The whole structure of Islam is based on the concept of *tawhid* which raises man to the highest and noblest rank. Significantly, Islam is referred to as the 'colour of Allah' (2:138) because it possesses a distinctive character and temperament. Islam strongly encourages creativeness: it does not put fetters on the mind with speculative philosophy or utopian ideals. It, however, elevates knowledge and learning to an act of worship.

It exhorts man to study and reflect and to make full use of his intelligence. The following verse reinforces man's approach to the unfolding of the cosmos:

"We shall show them Our signs on the horizons and within themselves..." (2: 30)

Shaykh Nadwi laments the fact that the Western nations have concentrated exclusively on material progress (*āfāq*) and have not directed their energies towards the secrets of the self, heart, and soul (*anfus*), through which they could have appreciated the grand design of creation. By the same token, they could have worked out a synergy of faith and natural progress. Shaykh

---

Civilisation, Islam and Muslims (Lucknow,1974), 9-32.
[62] Nadwi, *Muslims in the West*, 71.

Nadwi says:

> "Had a union taken place between the two, the history of mankind would have taken a different course. On the one side, the vast natural resources of America, the tremendous vitality, resolutions and enterprise of its people, on the other, the moderation of Islam, its message of hope and confidence, its unequalled distinction as the faith of nature and its insistence on the intrinsic innocence of man."[63]

Nadwi brings home an important truth: Islam strongly encourages creativeness in man and arouses his dormant capabilities. It is based on a robust sense of the realities of life that elevates learning to an act of worship. It calls on man to study and reflect, to make full use of his intelligence which is a Qur'anic imperative:

> "And in the earth are signs (*āyāt*) for those whose faith is sure, and (also) in yourselves. Can you not then see?" (51: 20-1)

In sum, Shaykh Nadwi broadens the scope of *da'wah* for the modern mind. He articulates a clear-cut message in the light of the following verses:

> "Do you not see how Allah has given the example of a good word? It is like a good tree, whose root is firmly fixed, and whose branches reach the sky, ever yielding it fruits in every season with the leave of its Lord. Allah gives examples for mankind that they may take heed." (14: 24-5)

A Qur'anic model as outlined in the above verses embrace time and space, and delineates the foundation and source of *da'wah*. No doubt, it is wedded to noble ideals and its message should reflect the purity of the 'good word'. More importantly, unless *da'wah* is presented "by someone who is illumined by inner light and conveyed with heartfelt conviction, it cannot bring about any change in the hearts and minds of the audience." To this end, the essence of *da'wah* should be reconfigured in the backdrop of sociopolitical changes.[64]

---

[63] Ibid., 86.
[64] Nadwi, *Islam in the West,* 10, 18.

Message for Muslims in the West

The Qur'anic model of *da'wah*, according to Shaykh Nadwi, is relevant to Muslims living across the world. Our focus is on Muslim immigrants who had settled in Britain and US after the World War II. Shaykh Nadwi's *da'wah* travels commenced in the 1960s when he served as an executive member of the Islamic Centre, founded by Sa'īd Ramadān in Geneva (Switzerland). His contributions to the magazine *Al-Muslimun* and lecture programmes paved the way for his regular *da'wah* programmes to Europe. His meetings with Muslims of different national and intellectual backgrounds who had settled in major cities like London and Berlin provided him with the opportunity to examine the potential of *da'wah* in the light of Qur'anic teachings.[65] Furthermore, Shaykh Nadwi explored the opportunities of communicating *da'wah* to non-Muslims in a coordinated way. This is not to suggest that Shaykh Nadwi encouraged polemical debates or interfaith dialogues by Muslims who had settled in these countries. Shaykh Nadwi viewed *da'wah* in the Qur'anic context as a critical tool to reach out to other faith groups through word and deed. In other words, Muslim communities had the great responsibility of communicating *da'wah* as outlined in the Qur'an and as transmitters of the Prophetic teachings. They were expected to internalise the Islamic values for others to emulate.

Shaykh Nadwi's evaluation of the Muslim commitment to Islam expresses his candour rather than a censure of the prevailing conditions in Muslim communities. He reminded Muslims to do introspection on their level of commitment to *da'wah* in light of the following verses:

"Shall We tell you of those who lose most in respect of their deeds? Those whose efforts have been wasted in this life, while they thought they were acquiring good by their works." (18: 103-4)

Shaykh Nadwi says:

"Be on your guard against this frame of mind and keep the security and preservation of faith above every kind of worldly success so that you do not depart from this world save as truthful Muslims. I say that a man who lives in America and takes the faith (*imān*) unimpaired

---

[65] Shaykh Nadwi's book *Speaking Plainly to the West* (1976) is a collection of lectures delivered in London and Berlin. Included in the book are articles submitted to the magazine *Al-Muslimun.*

with him to the next world will, perhaps, merit a greater reward than he who dies in Arabia because he protects the lamp of his faith against all sorts of storms and tempests."[66]

Shaykh Nadwi attempts to envision an ambitious *da'wah* model through which the Muslim communities may develop an outreach programme to preserve their Islamic presence in their respective countries. In contrast to the gloom or doom syndrome which characterises the vision of many 'ulama and preachers (*du'āt*) towards the West, Shaykh Nadwi is guided by the *wasatiyyah* approach: Muslims are expected to face the myriad of challenges in a constructive and pragmatic way.

Prerequisites: Islamic Leadership

In his lecture *Cultural Selfdom and Muslim Students*[67] Shaykh Nadwi makes a pertinent observation about the leadership crisis, which, by and large, had infiltrated Muslim countries. The Muslim leaders are products of Western universities but they are blind to the temperament and ideals of their own people to whom they return. They lack the power of faith because they cannot speak in the language of the Qur'an, which entails the highest degree of commitment and sacrifice. The integrational friction points to Muslims' abject surrender to the West. Leaders professing Islamic sentiments are in a denial mode. "Their bodies live in the East, their minds and souls in the West."[68] This view is further elaborated by Shaykh Nadwi:

Today too, our Muslims continue to possess the innate power of *imān*. Unfortunately, our leaders do not know the language of *imān*. Their intellect is only familiar with the language that verbalises their personal aspirations and expressions [which are distinctly un-Islamic]. However, they are not familiar with the language of the heart whose spontaneous and direct message may have (the desired effect). This language is linked to *imān*, Qur'an and the *Sahābah*.[69]

Shaykh Nadwi's address to the youth is explicit: leadership requires faith (*imān*) in the eternal teachings of the Qur'an and emulating the Prophetic model of excellence. The youth need to translate the Islamic ideals into the

---

[66] Nadwi, *Muslim in the West*, 158.

[67] Ibid.,173-83.

[68] Ibid., 180.

[69] Akram Nadwi, *Armughān i-Farang* (London, 2004), 92. Cf. Nadwi, *Towards Salvaging Humaniy*,128-38.

language of faith which draws its guidance from the Qur'an. Shaykh Nadwi's concern was that the Muslim students should be ambassadors of Islam in their respective communities. Their leadership roles must be *da'wah-* focused through establishing networks of Islamic activities and spreading the message of Islam to non-Muslims by employing the Qur'anic directives of wisdom (*hikmah*) and fair exhortation (*maw'izah*). In Shaykh Nadwi's words:

"Your stay in Europe or America is a unique opportunity from which you should derive the fullest advantage. Through it you can pave the way for the resurgence of Islam and the well- being of mankind. Your presence in these lands will be a source of strength to your faith; it will lead to trust and reliance on it, and new avenues for the programme of Islam will open as a result."[70]

Concluding Remarks

Shaykh Nadwi's perspectives on *da'wah* transcend his own sociopolitical experience and provides new insights into its adaptability within the global network. His focus on *da'wah* responsibilities is not confined to a traditional understanding of its scope and function; in fact, it is wide ranging and multifaceted and also shows a subtle shift to its dynamism and versatile style.

For Shaykh Nadwi, the Qur'an is the focal point of constructive *da'wah* from which flows the hierarchy of priorities and values, giving it a distinctive character. His approach covers a broad range of issues that shape the *da'wah* discourse in contemporary society.

Shaykh Nadwi had to develop the goals of *da'wah* through a structured methodology keeping in mind the different temperament and orientation of his audience. According to Shaykh Nadwi, *da'wah* is not a set of theoretical assumptions; rather it is a synergy of faith and action that is a principal agent of change. In this regard, the moral and social transformation are key elements in Shaykh Nadwi's presentation of *da'wah*.

---

[70] Nadwi, *Muslims in the West*, 191.

CHAPTER 2

Towards the Renewal of Islamic Thought

Islam and *Tajdīd*: Contemporary Framework

Contemporary Islamic thought is located in specific historical and political settings. Thus, the contributions of Shaykh Nadwi and his contemporaries reflect a variety of responses shaped by their respective understanding of *islāh* and *tajdīd* which underpin the trends of Islamic resurgence. In our examination of Shaykh Nadwi's writings, specific sources relating to his Qur'anic studies are explored.

Shaykh Nadwi's discussion of *tajdīd* is expressed in his multivolume *Saviours of Islamic Spirit*. The *islāhi* (reformist) element which is examined in the lives of *mujaddids* is a shared characteristic in Shaykh Nadwi's other writings dealing with biographies of scholars largely drawn from the Indian subcontinent.[1] According to Shaykh Nadwi, the *tajdīd* tradition is infused with the dynamic spirit of Islam. This tradition of struggle against unislamic practises, the spirit to persevere and restore the pristine teachings of the faith and the effort to reassert the divine message are as old as Islam itself.

The continuity of *tajdīd* implies that Islam has not suffered any rupture in terms of its reformatory endeavours during the past 1400 years. By the same token, Shaykh Nadwi expresses his candour about the emergence of heretical movements during these centuries which had threatened to stifle Islam. It was, however, the efforts of the *mujaddids* who "defended Islam against philosophies and schools of thought incompatible with it."

A prominent feature of Shaykh Nadwi's portrayal of the *mujaddids* is his reference to those 'ulama and *sufis* who Habibul Haq Nadvi regard as political positivists.[2] This term is intended to highlight the 'ulama's active role in the field of *jihād* and *tajdīd*, and perhaps negate the image built around them as being state functionaries. This view is elaborated in Shaykh Nadwi's widely acclaimed *Islam and the World*.[3]

The dominant theme of continuity in Islamic revivalism traces its roots to

---

[1] For example, *Sirat i-Sayyid Ahmad Shahid* (Karachi, 1987).

[2] Habibul Haq Nadwi, *Islamic Resurgent Movements in the Indo-Pak Subcontinent* (Durban, 1987), 37-8, 51-2.

[3] The importance of *Islam and the World* in the Arab Islamic reformist thought is expressed in Abu Rabi` Ibrahim, *Intellectual Origins of Islamic Resurgence in the Modern Arab World* (New York, 1996).

the *Sahābah* who were aptly described as the Qur'anic generation.[4] It must be noted that the revelation of the Qur'an did not operate in a vacuum; its dynamic influence was interiorised by the *Sahābah* under the guidance of the Holy Prophet (peace be upon him). Their total engagement with the Qur'an in relation to its universal teachings brought about a revolutionary change in human history.

Thus, it was that the most remarkable change brought about in human history. The Holy Prophet (peace be upon him) uncovered rich treasures of human material that had been lying dormant under the mass of Ignorance since the beginning of creation and imparted to them the light of genius which was to hold the world spellbound through ages to come. He had made into men what till then were mere herds of dumb driven cattle. He had aroused their innate possibilities; he had released the fountains of their real life and elevated them to the standard- bearers of light and learning and faith and culture in the world. Within a short span of time the desert of Arabia threw up mighty personalities whose names illumine the pages of history to this day.[5]

The term Ignorance (*Jāhiliyyah*)[6] referred to in the above extract is generally associated with the pre-Islamic period: its features embrace a litany of social and moral deterioration. Etymologically, the term *Jāhiliyyah* comes from the Arabic root (*jhl*).[7] For many a scholar *Jāhiliyyah* is antithetical to knowledge (*'ilm*). Turning to the Qur'an it may be used as a descriptive expression to denote a moral or social position.

In fact, the concept of *Jāhiliyyah* has several meanings due to its linguistic variation. In a particular sense the definition points out to the general characterisation of the people of Arabia. It is in the *Jāhili* poetry[8] that these attributes were embedded. Tribal prejudice, for example, dominated the Arab outlook on life. Combined with the Arab warlike temperament, it could provoke internecine wars with other tribes over trivial matters. The tribal conflicts served to perpetuate the culture of *Jāhiliyyah* in their lives.

It was the Qur'an that standardised the concept of *Jāhiliyyah*. It appears in several verses of the Qur'an with no specific reference to ignorance or lack

---

[4] Nadwi, *Islam and the World*, 53.

[5] Ibid, 71.

[6] Shaykh Nadwi's incisive analysis of *Jāhiliyyah* in a contemporary setting is discussed in *Islam and the World*, 45-50.

[7] Ibn Manzur, *Lisān al-'Arab*, vol.2 (Cairo, 972), 130-1.

[8] R. A. Nicholson, *A Literary History of the Arabs* (Delhi, 1996), 71-140.

of knowledge only. We may refer to two examples that support the variant meanings of this concept.

"Do not make a display of yourselves in the manner of the former *Jāhiliyyah*?" (33: 33).

Its social appeal is emphasised in this verse.

Many Islamists maintain that the following verse has a direct relevance to Islam's political position:

"Do they desire to be judged by the law of pagan ignorance (*hukm al-Jāhiliyyah*)? But for those who are firm in faith, who can be a better lawgiver than Allah?" (5: 50)

New *Jāhiliyyah*: Shaykh Nadwi's Critique

Shaykh Nadwi in his influential work *Islam and the World* sees the *Jāhiliyyah* of ancient Greece and Rome resurrected in modern Europe, and Muslim societies have become their allies and camp followers. Shaykh Nadwi states that the real fundamentals of the Greek civilisation were the rationalistic and eclectic spirit that pervaded its life. It prided itself in the field of philosophy and politics by producing intellectuals like Aristotle and Plato whose writings wielded a decisive influence on Islamic culture and civilisation. Nevertheless, Shaykh Nadwi asserts that the basic structure of the theological metaphysics of the Greeks left hardly any room for the development of the spirit of religious reverence and awe. This is evident in their repudiation of the Attributes of God and of His personal control of the universe, which he argues, could only lead to 'destruction of spirituality'.[9] The disregard for transcendental truths and its exaggerated emphasis of material comfort, described in detail by Shaykh Nadwi, have negatively impacted on the character of this great civilisation.

The Roman civilisation, according to Shaykh Nadwi, had never been a source of moral enthusiasm. Being wholly paganish and superstitious, it was incapable of checking skepticism and the spirit of disbelief among its followers. Consequently, as the Romans advanced culturally, they grew openly contemptuous of their faith. Materialism combined with aggressive

---

[9] Nadwi, *Islam and the World*, 113-9. For a new translation of Shaykh Nadwi's magnum opus, see *Rise and Fall of Muslims: Its Impact on the World* Spring (2020).

imperialism was the benchmark of its civilisation. A natural corollary of the materialism of the Romans was the exploitation of the weaker nations for selfish motives. Shaykh Nadwi observes that these characteristics have been inherited by modern Europe. He is also critical of Muslim societies that have absorbed the *Jāhili* traits of Western civilisation which in turn was influenced by the Greek and Roman civilisations. Abdur Raheem Kidwai makes a trenchant criticism about the rebranded *Jāhiliyyah* in the Arab world, and most Muslim countries:

"The region is regrettably under the grip of the very *Jāhiliyyah* against which Nadwi warns so eloquently while graphically citing the instructive examples of pagan Greece in the opening chapter of his work. His ken of critique is breathtakingly sweeping: he identifies the causes of the decline and fall of the Jews, Persians, Buddhists and Indians in the pre-Islamic days. In the vein of Gibbon, Toynbee and Durant, he ascribes the fall, in the main, to moral degeneration, social injustice and godlessness which were rife in these civilisations."[10]

However, Shaykh Nadwi has resisted generalising the Muslim community as embracing *Jāhiliyyah* in totality, a position assumed by some of his contemporaries. Shaykh Nadwi argues in his *Saviours of Islamic Spirit* that in Islam there has been a continuity of reformative (*tajdīdi*) movements and that there were no long intervals of inaction in Islamic history.[11]

In contextualising the *islāhi* contributions of the eminent historical figures selected by Shaykh Nadwi, the following essential points are to the fore:

- [The] primacy of the Qur'an and sunnah was embedded in their formulation of Islamic resurgence.
- They formed a link to the golden chain (*silsalah al-dhahab*) of the Islamic legacy that has over the centuries preserved its culture and civilisation.
- Their efforts to preserve the authenticity ideals served as a bulwark against embellished accounts spawned by heretical movements and politicised figures serving their vested interests.[12]

---

[10] Abdur Raheem Kidwai, "Rise and Fall of Muslims: Its Impact on the Muslim World," in *The Muslim World Book Review,* 40:3, 2020.

[11] Choughley, *Islamic Resurgence,* 197-22.1.

[12] Nadwi, *Saviours of Islamic Spirit,* vol. 1, 3-4.

According to Shaykh Nadwi, the Islamic renewal project has consistently portrayed the Qur'anic vision and Prophetic teachings in different times and under different circumstances. The *mujaddids* had shown resilience during critical periods in history when Islam was under threat by hostile forces seeking to undermine and in many instances eradicate its authenticity. This term has several implications: it is a key element in Shaykh Nadwi's conceptual framework of Islamic resurgence. Its parameters are clearly defined and as such Islamic reformers with *tajdīdi* and *islāhi* credentials are selected in his celebrated multivolume work.[13]

Shaykh Nadwi argues that the *tajdīdi* movements possess a vitality and relevance that demonstrate the completeness of Islam as a *dīn* which is highlighted in the following Qur'anic verse:

> "This day I have perfected for you your religion and have bestowed upon you My Bounty in full measure and have been pleased to assign for you Islam as your religion." (5: 3)

The divine arrangements for the existence of Islam are provided in several ways among which are the uninterrupted contributions of the 'ulama and *mashā'ikh* of incomparably high character and calibre.

Mujaddids: Saviours of Islamic Spirit

We now turn to three reformers drawn from different social milieu who left a lasting impression on the Islamic reformist thought. Our account deals with the following luminaries whose Qur'anic insights and contributions changed the course of Islamic history.

Shaykh 'Abdul Qadir Jilani

A scion of the Holy Prophet (peace be upon him) family, Shaykh 'Abdul Qadir Jilani (d. 1166) was a towering figure among the *mashā'i'kh* and a celebrated scholar whose writings continue to be read and taught over the centuries. The glowing account provided by Shaykh Nadwi is a conspectus of

---

[13] Muhammad Qasim Zaman, *The Ulama in Contemporary Islam: Custodians of Change* (Princeton, 2007), 170-3.

the abiding legacy of this preeminent reformer.

The reformers and renewers of faith succeeded in reviving the true faith and tapping new sources of popular strength in their own times through this tried and unerring method, which merely copied the procedure and technique of the Messenger of Allah. Countless individuals have not only been provided the opportunity to adopt a virtuous life through this method, but have been led to attain the stage of 'reality of faith' (*haqiqat al-imān*) and of 'beautification and excellence' (*ihsān*) by inspired guides and mentors, of whom the exemplar of the time was Shaykh 'Abdul Qadir Jilani. The history of peoples subscribing to the faith of Islam will bear witness that no guide with an illuminated soul was more successful than the Shaykh in bringing about a revival and resurgence of the true Islamic spirit.[14]

According to Shaykh Nadwi, the Shaykh's powerful sermons[15] were a source of inspiration to innumerable people in Baghdad. As a *mujaddid* he succeeded in reviving the true faith that provided an opportunity for countless people to lead a virtuous life. The Shaykh's moral excellence was defined by his total attachment to the Qur'anic teachings which he translated as gems of spiritual guidance for the masses. He was gifted with divine grace and illumination for which the Qur'an served as an unerring guide. His lessons on the Qur'an focused on *tawhid*, sunnah and on issues of the day.

Shaykh Nadwi makes copious reference to the Shaykh's notable collection of sermons to highlight the primacy of the Qur'an and self-reformation. For example, the love for Allah to the exclusion of everything else is succinctly described in the following words:

> "Keep your eyes fixed on Him Who is looking at you. Keep yourself before One Who keeps Himself before you. Love Him Who loves you. Listen to Him Who calls you. Seek help from Him Who can save you, take you out of the darkness of ignorance, cleanse you of the impurity of your soul, and redeem you from yourself and misleading temptations, despair and timidity... How long would you remain slaves of your desires, temptations, greed, pride–in short, this transitory world?"[16]

The Shaykh used to teach daily lessons on the topics of *tafsīr*, hadīth and

---

[14] Nadwi, *Saviours of Islamic Spirit,* vol.1, 179.
[15] The multivolume *Al-Fath-al-Rabbāni* is a treasure trove of sermons for seekers in the spiritual path.
[16] Nadwi, *Saviours of Islamic Spirit,* vol. 1, 178.

jurisprudence, in which he explained the various juristic schools of thought. The classes were generally held in the morning and evening, and the Shaykh listened to the recitation of the Qur'an after midday prayers, and thereafter dictated rulings (*fatwās*) or other *shar`i* matters referred to him.[17]

Shaykh Nadwi's inspiration to work out his own blueprint for the reform of Muslims finds resonance in the life and times of the Shaykh.

As an eminent man born to Islam [his] miracle of miracles lays in his inspiring and impressive teachings, which caused thousands to turn away from the lust of power to inculcate the true spirit of faith through self-correction and purification of the soul in an age of crass materialism.[18]

The Payām (referred elsewhere in the volume) illustrates in a different social milieu, the innate power of Islam to pursue goals of moral regeneration as was the case of the Shaykh. Also, the *tawhīd* articulation underscored by the Shaykh's spellbinding sermons suggested a template for Shaykh Nadwi to frame his methodology in the context of un-Islamic influences prevailing in the subcontinent. Reference may be made to the entrenched shrine-based rituals, for example, which are in direct conflict with the pristine form of *tawhīd*.

The Shaykh's enduring legacy across the Muslim world is representative of the *tajdīdi* trends that finds expression in the Islamic movements sharing similar ideals.

Ibn Taymiyyah

A preeminent figure in Islamic reformist thought, Ibn Taymiyyah[19] was a rare prodigy. His encyclopaedic knowledge and independent views contributed immensely to the *tajdīdi* tradition in which the Qur'an and sunnah constituted its intellectual base.

Shaykh Nadwi maintains that Ibn Taymiyyah stands out as the "greatest thinker and reformer in Islam whose influence extends to almost every reformative movement started since the eight century, and particularly to those which gained impetus during the twelfth century of the Islamic era."

Two distinctive qualities set Ibn Taymiyyah apart from the 'ulama establishment: first, he was a strong advocate fora reform of the administration in the spirit of the shari'ah. Second, he claimed the right of

---

[17] Ibid., 167.

[18] Ibid. 199-200.

[19] For a biographical account of the Ibn Taymiyyah, see Nadwi, *Saviours of Islamic Spirit,* vol. 2 (Lucknow, 1974), 3- 146.

ijtihād and used his independent judgement in reasserting the general principles of the Qur'an and sunnah.[20]

Shaykh Nadwi reviewed Ibn Taymiyyah's prolific service to Islam in five areas:

- Revival of the concept of *tawhīd* in its unadulterated form.
- Critique of philosophy, logic and *kalām* (theology).
- Promoting the methodology of the Qur'an and sunnah vision vis-à-vis other systems.
- Refutation of Islamic sects and deviant movements.
- Revival of the sciences of shari`ah and Islamic thought[21].

In the Qur'anic field, Ibn Taymiyyah's contributions are significant. His phenomenal memory was evident in his extensive study of *tafsīr*. He was endowed with a reflective mind to unravel the meaning and essence of the Qur'an. Shaykh Nadwi recounts Ibn Taymiyyah's extraordinary zeal to understand the content and substance of a single verse by consulting as many as one hundred *tafsīr* works.[22] Likewise, his introduction to the principles of *tafsīr* has attracted scholarly study in the Arab world.[23]

His commentary particular *surahs* and verses, Shaykh Nadwi opines, "restates the abiding truths in terms of life and surrounding conditions, make a close study of the different sections of society, their morals and customs.... [They] point out distorted innovations (*bid`ah*) in form and thought that result from the disregard of divine guidance (*hidāyah*)."[24]

Shaykh Nadwi's admiration of Ibn Taymiyyah's *tafsīr*, which has survived in a fragmented form,[25] is recognized for "its comprehensiveness, reformative zeal and a deepening sense of interpreting the Qur'an according to the current needs of the time."

---

[20] These two qualities are elaborated in M.M. Sharif, *A History of Muslim Philosophy*, vol. 2 (Karachi, 1983) 796-819.

[21] Akram Nadwi, *Shaykh Abul Hasan*, 135.

[22] Nadwi, *Saviours of Islamic Spirit*, vol. 2, 23.

[23] See Muhammad ibn Salih al-Uthaymin's explanation of this important work (London, 2014).

[24] Nadwi, *Saviours of Islamic Spirit*, vol. 2, 140.

[25] *Bayān al-Tafsīr* in ten volumes is a recent collection of Ibn Taymiyyah's *tafsīr* culled from his writings.

Chapter 2
Towards the Renewal of Islamic Thought

It is outside the scope of this study to examine in detail Ibn Taymiyyah's impact on the various Islamic movements, both orthodox and modernist, who drew upon their inspiration from the great reformer. Khaliq Ahmad Nizami's insightful paper, *The Impact of Ibn Taymiyyah on South Asia* is a summative assessment of his major influence in this region. Here mention may also be made of Ibn Taymiyyah's influence on Shaykh Nadwi. Several of his other writings reflect his praise of Ibn Taymiyyah's intellectual contributions and this perhaps has led his critics to label him a *salaf*. Nizami's remarks about Shaykh Nadwi's position in this regard are indicative of the latter's pragmatism on several contentious issues: "He (Shaykh Nadwi) propagated Ibn Taymiyyah's ideology without bringing it into clash with the religious psychology of the Muslims in South Asia."[26]

It will be not be out of place to refer to the seminar on Ibn Taymiyyah's contributions to the Islamic revivalist trends held at Jami'ah Salafiyyah (Varanasi) in 1987. As a keynote speaker, Shaykh Nadwi delivered a paper about Ibn Taymiyyah's stance on the core doctrines of Islam.[27]

Shaykh Nadwi brought into bold relief Ibn Taymiyyah's comprehensive discussion of *tawhīd* which serves as a locus on which other aspects of faith converge. His own writings emphasise the importance of *tawhīd* in response to the distorted version advanced by pseudo-sufis and deviant scholars. Similarly, Shaykh Nadwi discusses the concept of Prophethood in the writings of Ibn Taymiyyah which provide cogent proofs on the nature and function of divine revelation (*wahy*). For Shaykh Nadwi, Ibn Taymiyyah's critique of Greek philosophy exposes the hollowness of its metaphysical thought. Its intellectual inadequacies are critically examined. The limitation of the intellect, Shaykh Nadwi argued, is in direct contradiction of divine revelation which is the only infallible guide for a correct understanding of the cardinal doctrines of Islam. Shaykh Nadwi's assessment of Greek metaphysical thought is also brought out in a slim volume *Religion and Civilisation*.[28] The imprints of Ibn Taymiyyah and Al-Ghazali's contributions in this realm are reinforced in this concise work. At the same time, Shaykh Nadwi's insightful analysis on the characteristics of the Prophetic teachings (sunnah) in the light of *wasatiyyah* as a Qur'anic dictum is revealing. He touches on a social order that fits seamlessly into the Islamic civilisation ideal. This implies the rejection of Western civilisation

---

[26]Khaliq Ahmad Nizami, *On Islamic History and Culture* (Delhi, 1995), 76-113.

[27] Nadwi, *Kārwān*, vol. 3, (Lucknow, 1988), 325-32.

[28]Nadwi, *Religion and Civilisation* (Lucknow, 1975), 14-27.

and its trappings of a materialistic outlook.[29] The moral compass, Shaykh Nadwi insists, are the Prophetic teachings embedded in a *tajdīdi* framework over the centuries.

Shah Waliyullah

Among the intellectual figures of the subcontinent, Shah Waliyullah (d. 1762), emerges as an original thinker in the religio-academic renaissance of the Muslims of South Asia. According to Muhammad Ghazali, Shah Waliyullah was profoundly influenced by Ibn Taymiyyah and paid rich tributes to his scholarship and his typical revolutionary orthodoxy.[30] Similarly, citing Ibn Taymiyyah, Shaykh Nadwi attempts to show the common grounds between the *tajdīdi* endeavours of both Ibn Taymiyyah and Shah Waliyullah.[31]

The impact of the Shah on Shaykh Nadwi's important writings that deal with *tajdīd* is evident. In his *Saviours of Islamic Spirit* which is devoted to the life and thought of the Shah, Shaykh Nadwi's critical analysis of the latter's intellectual legacy is explored. The affinity of ideas in relation to the Qur'an and reformulation of Islamic thought in conspicuous in their respective writings.

Needless to add, Shaykh Nadwi's writings on Qur'anic studies and *tajdīd* owe a measure of debt to the Shah. Consider Shaykh Nadwi's formative years as a lecturer at Nadwah. Among other scholarly works, *Al-Fawz al-Kabir* was consulted to understand the Shah's methodology on the principles of *tafsīr*. For several years Shaykh Nadwi taught the Shah's magnum opus *Hujjat Allah al-Biiligha*[32] which was also praised in the Arab world. In Shaykh Nadwi's estimation, the *Hujjat* is a comprehensive work presenting a synthesis of `aqidah, social mores, economic guidelines, morality, statecraft and spirituality. It laid the foundation of a new theology (*kalām*) for the modern age of reason. More importantly, it is also an exposition of the shari'ah and *hadīth* derived from the prevailing circumstances during the

---

[29] Ibid., 108-12.

[30] Muhammad Ghazali, *The Sociopolitical Thought of Shah Wali Allah* (Islamabad, 2001).

[31] Nadwi, *Saviours of Islamic Spirit,* vol. 4, (Lucknow, 1993), 94-6.

[32] Waliyullah's magnum opus has been translated into English by Marcia Hermansen, *The Conclusive Argument of God* (Islamabad, 2003).

turbulent political period of Muslim rule in the subcontinent.

The central theme of social and political reform is expressed in the other writings of the Shah. His critique of the 'ulama, state officials and the masses reveal his deep insight into the society groping in ignorance, vice and political instability. Shaykh Nadwi shares Sayyid Abul Ala Mawdudi's (d. 1979) assessment about the significance of the Shah's reformative endeavours:

> "[The] Shah's works show how deeply he had pondered over the social conditions of the Muslims of his day. Such a critique necessarily creates an anxiety for reform ... and to draw a distinction between the wholesome and harmful custom usages. [The] urge for reform and regeneration is to chart out a well-defined programme for the reconstruction of society for giving it a correct direction. This is what we find the Shah doing with complete precision according to a comprehensive plan present in his critique of the Muslim society. Two points emerge from the Shah's *tajdīdi* endeavours: reconstruction of Muslim society and the demonstration of the foundational sources of Islam on the intellectual terrain."[33]

Shaykh Nadwi's writings on the reconstruction of the Muslim society are inspired by the Shah's critique albeit in a different setting. In *Basis of a New Social Order* Shaykh Nadwi explains the concept of wealth, for example, in the Islamic social order. Like the Shah, Shaykh Nadwi provides the rationale for wealth distribution so that an egalitarian society can be established. The following comment encapsulates this ideal:

> "In the Muslim society there is a greater scope for the promotion of social justice and other laudable social and moral ideals because of the instinctive respect it has for the Islamic way of life. [There] is the existence of the spiritual connection which has invested its diverse elements with a sense of identity and brotherhood."[34]

---

[33] Nadwi, *Saviours of Islamic Spirit*, vol.4, 247.
[34] Nadwi, *Basis of a New Social Order* (Lucknow, n.d.), 19.

A pioneering work in the Qur'an translation project, is the Shah's translation of the Divine Book into Persian. Shaykh Nadwi explains in detail the motivation for such a momentous undertaking. The subcontinent had used Persian as an official language which was patronised by Muslim dynasties. Arabic was linked to a formal acquisition of knowledge of Islamic disciplines through which the 'ulama exercised their religious autonomy. Under these circumstances, the masses remained ignorant of the teachings of Islam. By and large, syncretic practices permeated their religious thought; even a semblance of Islamic identity was tainted with a litany of un-Islamic practices.

According to Shaykh Nadwi, the Shah must have keenly felt the difference between the authentic teachings of the Qur'an and the practices of the Indian Muslims during his prolonged stay in Makkah. Moreover, it was a self-evident reality that *tawhīd* and *shirk* could not be expounded more forcefully and convincingly by anything than the Qur'an itself.[35]

The Persian translation and commentary of the Qur'an made its teachings accessible to the masses. It was, no doubt, a radical departure from superficial interpretations accumulated over the centuries which had created an impenetrable barrier to a direct understanding of the text.

The subsequent Urdu translations of the Qur'an by the sons of the Shah gained considerable acceptance in the subcontinent.[36] We may refer to the *Mudih al-Qur'ān* by 'Abdul Qadir Dehlawi (d. 1824). His mastery over Arabic and other Islamic disciplines was recognised by his contemporaries. In his *Foreword* Dehlawi introduces his Urdu translation as follows:

> "The language of the Qur'an is Arabic and an Indian cannot comprehend it as such. Therefore, as my father Shah Waliyullah translated it into Persian, I thought of rendering it into comprehensible language. The first point is that it is not a word to word translation because Urdu and Arabic are two different languages in grammar and usage. The second point is that the language of this translation is not rhetorical but simple and commonly used so that everyone can comprehend it."[37]

---

[35] For a summarised account in the Persian translation, see Nadwi, *Saviours,* vol. 4, 98-103.

[36] Ibid., 104.

[37] Cited in Nazeer Ahmad Ab. Majeed (ed.), *Quran Interpretation: A Critical Study* (New Delhi, 2019), 3.

The Qur'an as a Self-Study Guide

Shaykh Nadwi's approach to the study of the Qur'an merits attention. A faith, divine teachings, or call to noble ideals cannot exist in a vacuum. The history of religions and morality has shown how mankind spirals into degeneration without revealed guidance. Shaykh Nadwi makes an important remark that since the Qur'an has a universal dimension, it is therefore not restricted to an elitist group. Like the Shah, he reminds us that the path to guidance is to assimilate the teachings and the spirit of the Qur'an with an open mind.[38] In contrast, ignorance and prejudice are self-destructive tendencies that block a reverential approach to the divine Book. Likewise, Shaykh Nadwi states that the engagement with the text of the Qur'an should not be motivated by a judgmental outlook. One should approach it as a living Book meant for one's own reform. One should look for self-development in it before prescribing it for others.

In line with Shah's pioneering contribution to Qur'anic studies, Shaykh Nadwi broadens the scope of the Qur'anic ideals to specific conditions. His comments on the following verse are reflective of his insight into its contextual relevance:

> "It was not necessary for the believers to go forth together (to receive religious instruction); but why did not a party of them go forth that they may grow in religious understanding (*tafaqquh*), and that they may warn their people when they return to them, so that they may avoid (erroneous attitude)?" (9: 122)

For Shaykh Nadwi, faith should be maintained and at the same time should provide intellectual leadership. Pious scholars ('ulama) should carefully evaluate new developments and appreciate new demands. They should meet these demands while adhering to the spirit of the faith and the shari`ah. In this lies the meaning and scope of *tafaqquh*. The next stage in this direction is of *ijtihād* which calls for specialised qualification.

The term *tafaqquh* yields variant meanings in the context of the Qur'an and shari'ah. Shaykh Nadwi's grasp of the intricacies and rationale of the shari'ah are derived from this Qur'anic term.[39] Likewise, his brilliant exposition of the four pillars of Islam[40] share the following characteristics

---

[38] Nadwi, *Guidance fom the Holy Qur'ān*, 173.

[39] Ibid., 122.

[40] Nadwi, *The Four Pillars of Islam* (Karachi, 1988).

which are reflective of his scholarly temperament:

- Independent study of the Qur'an and *hadīth* literature which has a correlation with the subject matter.
- Comparative study and philosophy of worship in other faiths.
- Discussion of the underlying wisdom in respect of the four fundamental obligations based largely on the writings of the Shah.
- Presentation of the subject matter in modern idiom for the benefit of present day Muslims.[41]

By all accounts, *The Four Pillars of Islam* has been classified as an influential contribution to the field of *iqh* (Islamic jurisprudence). It is free from apologia and polemical approach. Additionally, it does not suffer from the traditional blemish of sterile legal issues and minute details of formal ritual.

---

[41] Ibid., vii-ix.

CHAPTER 3

Contemporary Islamic Thought

Qur'anic studies in the twentieth century witnessed a spate of writings dealing with themes that elicited a wide spectrum of views that represented the intellectual milieu in which Shaykh Nadwi was an influential figure. His writings in Arabic prefigured his calibre as a Qur'anic scholar who was engaged in presenting the perennial message of the sacred text to the modern man. Apart from his seminal works dealing with Islamic civilisation and the future destiny of the *ummah*, Shaykh Nadwi made invaluable contribution to the tafsir genre. In the main, he advocated a broader framework for interpreting the Qur'anic text within the mainstream definition.

Surah Al-Kahf: Meaning and Message

Shaykh Nadwi's original contribution to Qur'anic studies may be gleaned from his monographs and books devoted to specific *surahs*. Take for example, *Faith versus Materialism*.[1] As the subtitle suggests, it is the message of *Surah Al-Kahf* which is examined in this important work. The main themes have an organic unity in the *surah*: conflict between faith and materialism.[2] The study does not claim to be a commentary on the *surah*; instead, its contextual relevance is highlighted for readers who wish to draw guidance from the timeless message of the Qur'an.

For Shaykh Nadwi, the *surah* opened "[the] vista of a new world, conveying a range of meanings, yet unknown to me, pertaining to the same topic which can be termed as the struggle between faith and materialism." Its graphic descriptions symbolise a godless civilisation embodying traits of deception, denial of the overlordship of Allah and defying the political power of the day. According to Shaykh Nadwi, the *surah* also portrays the battle between two ideologies whose value systems are diametrically opposed to each other.[3]

Viewed from another angle, the *surah* brings into broad relief the limitation of human knowledge. For the Western mind or individuals inclined to liberal thought, their concept of knowledge hinges on their

---

[1] Nadwi, *Faith versus Materialism* (Lucknow, 1976).

[2] Ibid., 4.

[3] Ibid., 11-5.

capacity to probe the workings of the vast universe, plumb directly the secrets of the creation of life, and unlock the mysteries of the past and the future. In other words, this mindset boastfully claims to be the repository of knowledge for which revealed guidance is inconsequential.

Nadwi contends that the domain of human knowledge is prone to be utilised by vested interests for the purpose of exploiting vulnerable human beings. Capitalism, Communism and Socialism are appendages of an 'aberrant human nature'[4] which have devastated the earth's natural resources, fomented conflicts among nations and deepened social anarchy. By contrast, true faith is set out clearly in the parables of the *surah*. It emphasises the notion of divine knowledge (*ma'rifah*) that impels man to acknowledge the finitude of his knowledge. Hence, the need for true guidance through *wahy*. The following verse reinforce this assessment:

> "And if the all the trees in the earth were pens, and the sea, with seven more seas to help it (with ink), the Words of Allah could not be exhausted. Indeed, Allah is Mighty, Wise." (31: 27)

The *surah*, according to Shaykh Nadwi, reaffirms an important lesson that is interlinked with the Afterlife: "It calls upon us to keep this fundamental truth in view and draw inspiration from it in all our actions and behaviour." Overall, it offers an invaluable insight into its concluding verses:

> "And whoever hopes for the meeting with his Lord, let him do righteous work and make none the sharer of worship due unto his Lord." (18: 110)[5]

The book *Faith versus Materialism* was intended for a readership which had grown disillusioned with the pervasive influence of Westernisation. Therefore, Shaykh Nadwi's analytical approach to the contents of the *surah* is a timely response to the grave consequences of materialism that have seeped into Muslim countries.

Two distinguishing features mark out the book as an essential study to *tafsir*. First, Shaykh Nadwi does not follow the traditional pattern of Qur'anic commentaries as was done by Mawlana Manazir Ahsan Gilani (d.

---

[4] Ibid., 118.
[5] Ibid., 121.

1956)[6] who served as Head of Theology Department at the Osmania University (Hyderabad). On the contrary, the philosophical underpinnings and intellectual movements are closely examined by Shaykh Nadwi to assess, in the light of Prophetic language, the rise and decline of Western civilisation.[7] Second, Shaykh Nadwi's critical study of historical sources relating to incidents and legendary figures described in the *surah* reinforces his proficiency in comparative religion and universal history. This critical acumen can also be attributed to Daryabadi's mentoring role of understanding the genesis of Western civilisation. Shaykh Nadwi is able to draw independent conclusions, and augment his well- documented study on the contents and essence of the *surah*. His scholarship is also accentuated by way of selectivity. For example, the issue of the identification of Dhul Qarnain, has produced divergent opinions drawn from various historical sources. However, Shaykh Nadwi supports his views by citing the detailed explanation of Sayyid Qutb (d. 1966) in his celebrated *Fi Zilāl al-Qur'ān*.[8]

"It is wrong to try to evaluate the Qur'an with reference to history. There are two obvious reasons for this. The first is the fact that history is a recent creation which has missed countless events in mankind's progress. The Qur'an tells us some of these events which remain totally unknown to history and historians. Secondly, even though history may record some of these events, it remains the product of human beings. Thus, it suffers from the shortcomings of human action, such as imperfection, error, distortion, etc. ... Hence, whatever is said about referring to history in order to evaluate the accounts given in the Qur'an cannot be admitted on the basis of the scientific rules adopted by people, let alone by Islam which states clearly that the Qur'an is the final arbiter."[9]

Shaykh Nadwi is a discerning Qur'anic scholar, noted for his wide reading of contemporary *tafsirs* in Arabic and Urdu. He concurs with Qutb on the hazards of projecting historical data as absolute truths. This approach, Shaykh Nadwi argues, marginalises the Qur'anic declaration being the

---

[6] On Gilani's writings, see Muhammad Zafiruddin Miftahi, *Hayāti- Mawlana Gilāni* (Karachi, 1994), 325-36.
[7] Abdul Majid Daryabadi, *Maktubāt i-Majidi*, vol. 3 (Kolkata, 2001),193-288.
[8] Translated by Adil Salahi under the title *In the Shade of the Qur'ān* in 18 volumes by Islamic Foundation, Leicester.
[9] Qutb, *In the Shade of the Qur'ān*, vol. xi, 305.

'eternal, unchangeable word of Allah.'[10]

It is outside the scope of the study to examine the scholarly interaction between Qutb and Shaykh Nadwi. Nonetheless, Qutb's *Foreword*[11] and copious reference to *Islam and the Worl*[12] in his *tafsīr* is also a reaffirmation of Shaykh Nadwi's influential contribution to Qur'anic studies.

Farahi's Qur'anic Contribution

For a critical study of the eloquence of the Qur'an is Hamiduddin Farahi's (d. 1930) encyclopaedic work[13] on the coherence (*nazm*) in *surahs*. In Shaykh Nadwi's words:

> "[Farahi] gave origin to a new school of *tafsīr* by demonstrating the interconnectedness (*nazm*) between verses of the Qur'an and a pre-conceived pattern of the content and consistency of the message in the Scripture."[14]

As the founding father of Qur'anic hermeneutics, Farahi explored themes which had a *nazm* significance. Therefore, semantics embodied new approaches to grammatical construction that impacted on the nuanced interpretation of *i'jāz*. In more than one way, the Farahian methodology created a fundamental shift to a critical analysis of the sacred text. It attempted to locate the inner logic, syntactic structure, symmetrical design and flawless patterns of connectivity and coherence that was a lesser study area in the *tafsīr* tradition.

Abu Sufyan Islahi has correctly observed that the incremental interest in Farahi's Qur'anic contributions are now avidly studied and researched in the Arab world.[15]

Take for instance, the rhetorical usage of oaths (*aqsām*) in the Qur'an. It requires specialised knowledge to appreciate its literary merit and

---

[10] Nadwi, *Faith versus Materialism*, 87.

[11] Nadwi, *Islam and the World*, 1-6.

[12] See Qutb, *In the Shade*, vol. xv (Leicester, 2008), 162-3.

[13] For a brief biographical sketch on Farahi, see Amin Ahsan Islahi, *Tadabbur-e-Qur'ān*, vol.1. Translated by Muhammad Saleem Kayani (Kuala Lumpur, 2006), 667-71.

[14] Nadwi, *Islamic Studies, Orientalists and Muslims Scholars* (Lucknow, 1984), 49.

[15] Islahi, *Madrasat al- Islāh Fuzalii ki Qur'āni Khidmāt* (Aligarh, 2019), 10.

relevance from the Qur'anic perspective. Shaykh Nadwi's *Introduction*[16] is a synoptic assessment of this noteworthy work by Farahi and reflects his own versatility in the sciences of the Qur'an.

An erudite scholar, Farahi commanded knowledge of a number of languages among which were Hebrew and English. He also taught Arabic at Aligarh Muslim University. The study of the Qur'an was his forte and to this end his remarkable achievements added new dimensions to the literary and structural analysis of the Divine Book.[17]

Contemporary Approaches to the Qur'an: An Overview

Shaykh Nadwi's appreciation of Farahi's work stems from his lifelong association with Arabic literature. It is to Shaykh Nadwi's credit that seminars[18] were hosted to explore new trends of Qur'anic scholarship. His visionary leadership in Islamic literature (*adab*) encouraged leading scholars to undertake systematic and comparative researches in line with contemporary trends of interpreting the Qur'an. Needless to say, the reincarnation of Orientalism is now entrenched within the ranks of modernist Muslims and pseudo-intellectuals. Hermeneutics[19] now dominates the Qur'anic discourse. Terms like religio-ethical theories,[20] liberation theology[21] and gender equality[22] are enthusiastically promoted in order to undermine the relevance of the Qur'an for all times. Alongside this alarming trend, there has been a 'gradual, steady Muslim intellectual response, rather a rejoinder to the Orientalists attacks on the Qur'an.'[23]

Shaykh Nadwi's critique of the Orientalist project is summarised hereunder:

---

[16] Farahi, *Im'ān Fi Aqsām al-Qur'ān* (Damascus, 1994).

[17] For a useful study on Farahi's *nazm* theory, see Mustansir Mir, *Coherence in the Qur'ān* (Indianapolis, 1986).

[18] The *Karwān i-Adab* of the Rabita Adab contains insightful articles on the seminars organised by the organisation.

[19] On hermeneutics and the Qur'an, see Fazlur Rahman, *Revival and Reform in Islam* (Oxford, 2000), 9-23.

[20] See Abdullah Saeed, *Interpreting the Qur'ān: Towards a Contemporary Approach* (New York 2006).

[21] See Farid Esack, *Quran Liberation & Pluralism* (Oxford, 1997).

[22] For example, Asma Barlas, *"Believing Women in Islam": Unreading Patriarchical Interpretaions of the Qur'ān* (Texas, 2000).

[23] Kidwai, *Translating the Untranslatable*, xvii.

[They] spend their time and energy in identifying the flaws in shari'ah, Muslim history and culture. They project these flaws in a dramatic, horrible way. Their objective behind writing these books is to sow doubts in readers on the basis of their shrewd arguments against the Qur'an, *hadīth*, *iqh* and Islamic theology.[24]

While making a brief survey of the Orientalist production of Qur'anic translations and other Islamic disciplines, Shaykh Nadwi makes a two-fold observation: Muslim scholars should critically examine Orientalist writings and expose their misrepresentation of Islamic disciplines. To counter this menace, original works by Muslim scholars should be produced and excellent standards be maintained for the modern educated class.[25]

Daryabadi's *Tafsīr* Contributions

There are two distinct phases in Shaykh Nadwi's relationship with the illustrious scholar of Qur'anic studies, Mawlana Abdul Majid Daryabadi (d. 1977).[26] A translator of the Qur'an into English and Urdu as well as books dealing with specific aspects on the Qur'an, Daryabadi excelled contemporary translators in his mastery over comparative religious studies and an array of modern knowledge to which belong philosophy, psychology, and sociology.[27]

Shaykh Nadwi's interaction with Daryabadi dates back as early as the 1930s when the magazine *Sach/Sidq*[28] contained incisive papers on Western

---

[24] Bilal Abdul Hayy Nadwi, *Mawlana Sayyid Abul Hasan Ali Nadwi's Thought and Mission* (unpublished), 37-8.

[25] For a systematic critique of Orientalists scholarship in the field of Qur'anic studies, see Muhammad Mustafa Azami. *The History of the Qur'ānic Text From Revelation to Compilation* (Selangor, 2011).

[26] For a brilliant exposition of Daryabadi's life and thought, see Abdur Raheem Kidwai, *From Darkness into Light: Life and Works of Mawlana Daryabadi, 1892-1977* (Springs, 2013).

[27] Ibid., 102-70. Cf. Akhtarul Wasey and Abdur Raheem Kidwai (editors), *Journey of Faith: Maulana Abdul Majid Daryabadi* (New Delhi, 2016).

[28] Ibid., 84-101. The title of the magazine underwent significant changes: *Sach*, *Sidq* and *Sidq-i-Jadid* (1925-77). The format and content had a thematic coverage, keeping in mind the cross-currents of sociopolitical developments in the country.

civilisation. Shaykh Nadwi benefitted immensely from Daryabadi's insightful articles which provide Qur'anic perspectives on the emerging patterns of scholarship in the West and their concomitant encroachment in Muslim countries.

His correspondence with Daryabadi covered many aspects of *tafsīr*. According to Shaykh Nadwi, many passages of the Qur'an cannot be fully appreciated without a correct understanding of their circumstantial setting and historical context. Daryabadi's established reputation in Western learning guided Shaykh Nadwi to access sources directly for his *tafsir* teaching and later for his ground breaking work *Islam and the World*. His admiration for Daryabadi's *tafsīr* is clearly expressed in the following words. "In the light of my knowledge of the current scholarly activities in the field of the Qur'an, based on my visits to the Arab world, Europe and US, I affirm that Allah enabled an Indian scholar serving admirably the cause of Islam, Mawlana Darayabadi, to undertake an extensive, systematic study of comparative religions and of the early Scriptures. His *tafsīr* is a testament to his ambition and sincerity."[29]

Shaykh Nadwi's collaborative efforts to publish Daryabadi's *tafsirs* in English and Urdu through the Academy of Islamic Research and Publications (Lucknow) are illustrative of the latter's influence on his lifelong Qur'anic studies. Some of the distinctive features of Daryabadi's English translation are enumerated by Shaykh Nadwi:

"There was, however, the need for another English translation of the Qur'an complete with explanatory notes, which could be recommended with confidence to Muslims and non-Muslims. The author of such exegesis (*tafsīr*) inevitably had to expound the Qur'anic text in terms acceptable to the *Ahl-Sunnah wa al-Jamā'ah*; to avoid putting forward his own views and ideas into the exegesis...[and] to avoid an apologetic approach in expounding the Qur'anic injunctions and institutions.. [Taking] all these factors into account Abdul Majid Daryabadi's translation and commentary is undoubtedly unique and most acceptable among all the exegetical readings of the Holy Qur'an so far attempted in the English language. The exegesis by Daryabadi throws ample light on all those communities who have been mentioned in the Holy Qur'an along with their geographical locations and the eras in which they flourished. His exegesis also demonstrates in the light of human

---

[29] Kidwai, *From Darkness*, 128-9.

experience and researches made in the field of anthropology and sociology, the superiority of the Islamic social order…A distinguishing feature of [his] exegesis is that it provides a conclusive answer to those Jewish and Christian critics who claim that the Holy Qur'an draws its materials from the Scripture and apocryphal writings of Judaism and Christianity."[30]

Appreciative comments were received from the founder of the Jama'at i-Islami, Abul Ala Mawdudi concerning the proposed English translation by Daryabadi. He says:

"We endorse the view that a standard, reliable translation is the need of the hour for not only non-Muslim English readership, but also for another very large constituency comprising modern educated Muslims. They need it for gaining a correct understanding of Islam."[31]

A magisterial work of Daryabadi, the *tafsīr*, however, did not attract the interest of leading publishers presumably because he did not belong to any 'ulama establishment. Also sectarian bias delayed its publication. In 1939 the translation was ready for publication. The publisher, Taj Company, had undertaken its printing over a thirty-month instalment period. It was only in 1957 that the complete translation was made available. However, the work was marred by glaring errors and therefore did not enjoy wide publicity as intended. During this prolonged period, Daryabadi continued with his revision of the translation and incorporated new material from the latest research available. It was again at Shaykh Nadwi's behest that the Academy of Islamic Research and Publications published the work as *Tafsīr al-Qur'ān* between 1981-5. Also, at the behest of Shaykh Nadwi, the Islamic Foundation (Leicester, 2008) brought out a single volume edition of this work in 2001. The abridged edition contains the revised translation and appropriate selection of explanatory notes culled from Daryabadi's multivolume translation.[32]

Shaykh Nadwi's acknowledgement of the sources and eminent figures

---

[30] Abdul Majid Daryabadi, *The Glorious Qur'ān*, xxii – xxiv.
[31] Kidwai, *From Darkness*, 107-8.
[32] Ibid.,103-4.

who honed his skills in the *tafsīr* genre also reveals his stature as a leading scholar of Qur'anic studies. In Shaykh Nadwi's estimation, the perspectives of the Qur'an can be actualised in different circumstances and changing scenarios within a geopolitical setting. His unrelenting efforts to promoting the cause of Islam are directly linked to his prolific writings which are anchored on the Qur'an and the sunnah. Thus the progression of his Qur'anic contributions spans a timeline in which contemporary Islamic thought runs parallel to his visionary formulation of *da'wah*.

Muhammad Asad

Shaykh Nadwi was influenced by scholars beyond the subcontinent periphery. Muhammad Asad (d.1992) of Jewish origin was one notable example. His important works *Islam at the Crossroads* (1934) and *The Message of the Qur'ān* (1980) have earned him immortal fame in the Muslim world.

Asad's biography *The Road to Mecca* (1954) reveals the literary gems of his brilliance. Shaykh Nadwi's admiration of this biography was undeniable; in fact, an Urdu version was published by him. Also *Islam at the Crossroads* had a considerable impact on his critique of Western civilisation. In respect of Asad's *tafsīr*, Shaykh Nadwi stated that it did not meet the approval of Muslims as it tended to promote liberal views that were at odds with mainstream exegetical interpretation.[33]

---

[33] Cited in Choughley, *Islamic Resurgence*, 126-9.

CHAPTER 4

The Qur'anic Concept of Knowledge

The *Iqra* Paradigm: An Appraisal

Two major writings *Islam and the World* and *Western Civilisation Islam and Muslims* may be studied together in order to obtain a correct perspective of knowledge offered by Shaykh Nadwi. Also monographs[1] written for specific occasions detail Shaykh Nadwi's enlightened views about the purpose of knowledge within the Islamic framework. His contributions to this field have broadened our understanding of the Qur'anic representation of knowledge framed through the *iqrā* paradigm. Also a brief mention of Shaykh Nadwi's close association with universities suggest his initiatives to demonstrate Islam's enduring legacy in the field of knowledge and intellectual endeavours.[2]

Barely a year had passed after Shaykh Nadwi received the King Faisal Award (1980) when he was conferred a D. Litt (Doctor of Literature) in October 1981 by the University of Kashmir. Shaykh Nadwi's conditional acceptance of this prestigious award was unambiguous: no political agenda was to be attached to this conferment. Furthermore, he had several scholars before him who set the precedent in receiving honorary doctorates. The brief address which he delivered at the Seventh Convocation of the Kashmir University was widely appreciated. The audience which included critics, teachers and students and specialists in both the traditional (*qadim*) and modern (*jadid*) sciences were enthralled by his inspirational address. Shaykh Nadwi's preliminary remarks showed that knowledge was an organic unity, an integral whole, that could not be divided into parts and it was necessary to rise above the ramparts of bifurcated traditional and modern branches of study. His reference to the *iqrā* paradigm set the tone for this important address in which he called for the fusion of knowledge and action.[3]

According to Shaykh Nadwi, the first revelation was a remarkable event; it was an event of immense significance which had an important bearing on

---

[1] For example, the monograph *The Place of Knowledge and the Role of Scholars* (Springs, 2018) was a lecture delivered at the University of Kashmir in 1981.

[2] Ibid., 2.

[3] Nadwi, *Islam and Knowledge*, 2-3.

the life of humanity. The initial verses of the Qur'an commenced with the directive to read, and not with a command to worship Allah. The divine revelation changed not only the course of human history but it also transformed the fate of mankind. Implicit in this divine declaration was the foundation of knowledge, symbolised by the pen which would usher in an era of unprecedented transformation.[4] Nadwi makes an important assessment in this regard:

"It was a revolutionary message as mankind was instructed that knowledge should be pursued under the guidance of the All Wise, All Knowing Allah. For this journey of knowledge is long, drawn out and hazardous. It is very vulnerable, subject to various hazards and dangers. It is therefore essential that knowledge must be carried out under the guidance of a perfect mentor. Allah alone serves as the perfect mentor. Another equally significant point is that Islam does not stand for knowledge in its absolute sense. Thus cosmetic, trivial, quarrel some, confrontational, materialistic and mechanical forms of knowledge are not intended. Rather, the Qur'anic message is: "Read in the name of your Lord Who created. He created man from a clot of blood. Recite and your Lord is Most Generous. He taught by the pen. He taught man which he did know (96: 1-5)." The Qur'an revealed another radical and indubitable truth that knowledge is boundless. The Qur'an says that Allah taught man which he did not know. It embraces all advancements in science, technology, journey to space, and the present globalization (of the world). All expansion of knowledge is covered by the Qur'anic assertion that Allah has taught man all that which he did not know."[5]

Knowledge and Faith

For Shaykh Nadwi, Islam restored the link between man the Lord Who created all that exists. The command to read and acquire knowledge was moulded under the direct guidance of the divine Messenger and in the name of the Lord (*Rabb*) so that man may proceed in his journey which is illumined by an unerring faith. In his quest for probing the frontiers of knowledge man is constantly reminded that the acquisition of knowledge is derived

---

[4] Nadwi, *The Place of Knowledge*, 10-11.
[5] Nadwi, *The Place of Knowledge*, 7.

from the spirit of Allah- consciousness (*taqwā*). Therefore, faith is the harbinger of eternal truths and can only be understood in the context of divine revelation (*wahy*).

Shaykh Nadwi laments the fact that the acquisition of knowledge has produced negative results. Man has delinked himself from the responsibility of being a custodian (*khalifah*) of Allah, the Lord of the Worlds. He has been given charge of the world, not ownership. Tragically, it is his bloated ego and overweening ambition under the guise of personal, political and racial domination that have perpetrated "countless varieties of servitude, injustice and debasement of mankind."[6]

Shaykh Nadwi restates the nexus between knowledge and moral values. Knowledge sustained by Islamic higher objectives can save mankind from the perils of moral and spiritual ruin. By the same token, cardinal beliefs and core values like *taqwā*, love for humanity will channelise our thoughts and actions into constructive strategies. A rebellious spirit that seeks to undermine the worldview of Islam must be exorcised for the *ummah* to redeem itself from its past failures. The challenges posed by Western civilisation are not cast in iron mould. In the final analysis, the *ummah* can reframe its own destiny by benefitting from the technological gains of the West without compromising its noble pursuits.[7] For Nadwi, the Muslim world requires an overhaul of its fractious view of knowledge. The only realistic course for them is to make full use of science and technology from the West by realigning these to the lofty ideals of Islam. Again, he reminds Muslims that the title 'Best of the People' is not an entitlement but a value- driven vision that will ensure harmony and equilibrium for mankind. It is a broad definition which encapsulates the pursuit of knowledge spurred by moral ideals and not self-centric traits. In fact, the lost treasure (of knowledge) alluded by the Prophetic counsel has resonance for modern Muslims. In a contemporary setting, Shaykh Nadwi offers insightful thoughts about the Islam and West discourse.[8]

Integration of Knowledge

It is the integration of knowledge and faith which produced a galaxy of illustrious scholars, thinkers and writers of different branches of religious

---

[6] Nadwi, *Islam and Knowledge*, 9.
[7] Nadwi, *Western Civilisation*, 9-32.
[8] Ibid., 212.

and secular sciences. Guided by the true purpose of knowledge, Shaykh Nadwi says, Muslims not only "achieved political and intellectual supremacy and found extensive and large empires, but they also surpassed at one time, all other nations in the field of knowledge." In other words, the fusion of the sacred and the secular did not create a cleavage of worldly and otherworldly pursuits. 'Allāmah Iqbal (d. 1938) reinforced this notion in the following couplet:

Talk of modern and ancient
Is the sign of narrowness of vision

Shaykh Nadwi's admiration of Iqbal's poetry is reflected in his *Glory of Iqbal*.[9] The poet of the East's devotion and deep reflection on the sacred text is highlighted in his writings. His initial source of inspiration was his father' wise comment about the Qur'an: The Holy Book can 'reveal' itself to the readers according to their spiritual degrees.[10] This key insight was a catalyst for Iqbal's reverential approach to the sacred text. For him, the world of the Qur'an was not couched in technical niceties that tended to obscure its dynamic appeal.[11] Rather, the wisdom and guidance from the Qur'an is timeless. In the background of the Communist rise on the world scene, Iqbal advocated the Qur'anic teachings "which could bring about the spiritual evolution of the human beings enabling them to look at all the human societies as different segments of one expansive brotherhood."[12]

Through the medium of his soul-stirring poetry, Iqbal had aroused the collective conscience of the *ummah* to be wary of Western education which fragmented knowledge into a secular mould. Shaykh Nadwi praises the sublimity of Iqbal's art to highlight the prevailing intellectual crisis among Muslims, resulting from poor imitation of an educational system that is not compatible with the Islamic vision. The anomaly is best illustrated by the following parable:

"There is an oriental story that accurately depicts the pitfalls of an unwary foreign educational system: Once upon a time there was a great flood, and involved in the flood were two creatures, a monkey and a fish. The monkey being agile and experienced was lucky

---

[9] Nadwi, *Glory of Iqbal* (Lucknow, 1973).
[10] Khurram Ali Shafique, *Iqbal An Illustrated Biography* (Lahore, 2007), 19.
[11] Muhammad Munawwar, *Dimensions of Iqbal* (Lahore, 1986), 136.
[12] Ibid., 119.

enough to scramble up to a tree and escape the raging waters. As he looked down from his safe perch, he saw the poor fish struggling against the soft current. With the very best of the intentions he reached down and lifted the fish from the water. The result was inevitable."[13]

Iqbal and Shaykh Nadwi shared a common bond in respect of the Qur'anic worldview. For them, reflection (*tadabbur*) was a nodal point to interpret the centrality of the Qur'anic message for the modern mind. Likewise, Shaykh Nadwi benefitted immensely from Iqbal's poetical genius to critique Western civilisation. It was a cogent, well-structured critical appraisal that took into account the conflicting Muslim response to Western incursion. In sum, like Iqbal, Shaykh Nadwi advocated the reconstruction of Muslim society.

Shaykh Nadwi is among the leading scholars who have focused on the integration of the Qur'anic vision of knowledge for *madāris* and tertiary institutions offering Islamic studies. He maintains that the success of this project depends on levels of commitment by intellectuals and Islamic organisations. In sum, meaningful strategies and policies need to be adopted for their effective implementation in the fields of knowledge and intellectual endeavours. He strongly advances a Qur'an-inspired approach to the challenges spawned by Western civilisation. He outlines pragmatic and sustainable solutions to the crises affecting humanity based on a correct appraisal of divine revelation. There exists no contradiction in the pursuit of knowledge with a religious sanction. In fact, scientific advancement that flourished during the heyday of Islamic civilisation is a poignant reminder of the integration process.

Islamic Literature Renewal Project

Nadwah's reformatory initiatives of Arabic literature in its curriculum are generally associated with Shibli Nu'māni (d. 1914).[14] He was an illustrious figure among the 'ulama who envisaged the merger between Islamic and modern knowledge. It is to his credit that Arabic developed into a dynamic language as a literary vehicle to promoting the reformist vision

---

[13] Nadwi, System of Education in Muslim Countries, in *Al-Furqan* English Digest (1976), 62.

[14] For a comprehensive account of Shibli's life and thought, see Sulayman Nadwi, *Hayāt i-Shibli* (Azamgarh, 1943).

that Nadwah stood for. For Shaykh Nadwi,[15] this tradition was strengthened by his two teachers, Arab Sahib and Shaykh Taqi al-din Hilāli (d. 1987), a prominent scholar who made great strides to the growth and development of the Arabic language at Nadwah.

Commenting on the Arabic language, Shaykh Nadwi makes an important point:

> "In the company of (Hilāli), two realities unfolded before me for the first time: the difference between language and literature (*adab*). Language is the foundation of *adab*, which is the gallery of the former and adorns its walls with portraits. On the other hand, *adab* represents the highest form of expressions through which progressive thoughts serve as vehicle. Culture and ideals are sustained (by this genre)."[16]

Language is inextricably linked to literature and both are not mutually exclusive entities. Shaykh Nadwi provided a survey of the anomalous situation in India with regards to the teaching of Arabic in *madāris*. According to him, Arabic, as a dynamic language has been largely marginalised in these institutions and undue emphasis is given to grammar and a few classical texts which presumably are expected to build competence in a student.

Qasas Al-Nabiyyin: Stories of the Prophets

Shaykh Nadwi's debut in Arabic literature is evident from his widely acclaimed *Qasas Al-Nabiyyin*. As a masterpiece of children literature, the multivolume work has enjoyed enormous popularity in the Muslim world. Nadwah was constructively engaged in producing standard Islamic textbooks which reflected the Islamic ethos. The Arabic language and literature are the real treasures of Islamic knowledge and cultural heritage; hence, their importance in Nadwah's curriculum.[17]

The *Qasas* was an alternative to the textbooks procured from Egypt by Nadwah in its early years and were prescribed for honing the skills of students in spoken and written Arabic. According to Daryabadi, the contents of these

---

[15] For Hilali's literary influence on Shaykh Nadwi, see Nadwi, *Kārwān*, vol.1, 119-26.

[16] Nadwi, *Meri 'Ilmi*, 16.

[17] Rabey Nadwi, *An Eminent Scholar*, 132.

textbooks had a secular orientation, and had no "reference to Allah and His Messenger from the start to the end."[18]

During 1943-44, Shaykh Nadwi began with the *Qasas* series. The lives of the major Prophets were covered and their contributions to human civilisation and culture were briefly dealt with.

Prominent features of *Qasas al-Nabiyyin*:

- Qur'anic language and style is employed.
- The Islamic belief system (*tawhīd*, Prophethood, etc.) make up the core content of the work.[19] As a corollary, *kufr* and *shirk* which are antithetical to *tawhid*, are highlighted.

The *Qasas* was duly completed in 1977 with the life of the Holy Prophet (peace be upon him). The eminent scholar of Egypt, Sayyid Qutb made the following comment:

> "I testify without reservation, that Abul Hasan's present book surpasses all such works. What accounts for its excellence is the inclusion, with elucidation of subtle teachings of the Qur'an of explanations that highlight and reciprocate the Qur'anic message through the author's apt comments interwoven into the telling of the story."[20]

The distinguished Egyptian scholar, Ahmad Sharbasi, wrote his Introduction to the *Qasas* series. He commended Shaykh Nadwi for restoring the link between the Qur'an and children's literature. He was of the view that that the *Qasas* should be a prescribed textbook at schools in the Arab world. It also held a pride as a fountainhead of Islamic culture for the younger generation. Sharbasi believed that this work could create real opportunities of establishing networks across Muslim societies because it is based primarily on the Qur'an.

Several seminars had been hosted in recent years on Shaykh Nadwi's *Qasas* series in both Arabic and Urdu languages. The lectures in these seminars deal with Shaykh Nadwi's innovative contributions to the children literature. Of significance is the growing interest in this work among

---

[18] Nadwi, *Kārwān*, vol.1, 216.

[19] Ibid., 217.

[20] Nadwi, *Kārwān i-Adab* (Lucknow, 2001), 220-92; Nadwi, *Stories of the Prophets*, 7-8.

literary critics from other parts of the Muslim world. Translation of this work into major languages has continued during the last few decades.

The Qur'anic Dimensions of Literature

Shaykh Nadwi's literary influence extended to prestigious Arabic academies. Also, he presented his paper on the contours that shape Islamic literature at the Academy of Arabic Learning known as *Majma' al-'Ilmi al-Arabi.*[21] He maintained ties with many litterateurs who supported his vision and were eager to work on it.

The subsequent years saw the culmination of Shaykh Nadwi's unwavering efforts for the Islamic literature project. The World Forum of Islamic literature[22] was established in 1986. As President of the Forum, Shaykh Nadwi endorsed the role of Islamic literature inspired by the Qur'an and the Prophetic teachings. As the work progressed and gained recognition, Shaykh Nadwi's major contribution was widely acknowledged. According to him, literature began with the divine Scriptures and the Holy Qur'an inscribed the seal of perfection on them. The elevation of literature is pithily expressed in the following verse:

> "Indeed, this is a revelation from the Lord of the universe, which the truthful Spirit has carried down to your heart that you might become one of those who warn (others on behalf of Allah), (a revelation) in clear Arabic language." (26: 192-5)

As an accomplished writer and outstanding orator, Shaykh Nadwi together with other litterateurs worked tirelessly towards reaching out to a global audience for advancing the cause of Islamic literature. Its success growth was substantial and the number of conferences across the Muslim world served to enhance its important role. The *takrim* (honourable citation) sessions and special issues of journals[23] devoted to Shaykh Nadwi's writings were in recognition of his distinguished service to this genre.

---

[21] Rabey Nadwi, *An Eminent Scholar*, 134.
[22] Ibid., 130-40 on the establishment of the *Rābita Adab al-Islami al- 'Alami.*
[23] For example, the Arabic journal, *Al-Manhal.*

Islahi's insightful assessment[24] about Shaykh Nadwi's Qur'anic contributions makes interesting reading. The latter possessed a remarkable literary style that left a distinctive mark in his writings which were germane to the Qur'anic content. His linguistic expression and fluency of thought are located in the Qur'anic milieu. As a student of the sacred text Shaykh Nadwi contextualises verses to ground realities. Without compromising the norms of linguistic and exegetical requirements the Qur'anic teachings are clearly elucidated.

Shaykh Nadwi's mastery over Qur'anic Arabic illustrates his versatile approach to issues affecting the Muslim society. Take for example, 'the footsteps of Satan' (*khutuwāt al-Shaytān*). The grammatical construction, according to Shaykh Nadwi, covers a wide range of meanings that includes doctrinal, social, economic and political evil. In a similar vein, he expands the meaning of particular verses emphasizing the sanctity of human life.[25]

For the Indian society, Shaykh Nadwi makes an important statement about the concept of equality and humanity. Islam had brought this revolutionary message to the Indian soil in the early years of its presence. Needless to add, the charter of human rights is deeply embedded in the Qur'anic worldview.[26]

Locating the Qur'anic Message

Shaykh Nadwi's involvement in mainstream activities in the country was dictated by his overall concern to foster a culture of morality against the backdrop of sociopolitical challenges. His *Payām* established within the general guidelines of the Qur'an and sunnah was a moral compass for the Indian society. There was no explicit *da'wah*; instead, he couched the mission of the Prophets in contemporary idiom. This approach was amenable to other faith groups who saw the commonality of ideas in their circumstantial settings. The thrust of communal harmony was essentially supported by the Qur'anic teachings. As opposed to the superficial and other sectarian readings of the Qur'an by Islamic movements, Shaykh Nadwi believed in the restoration of moral values that served as a conduit for genuine transformation of the Indian society. His lectures and writings were translated into various languages to disseminate the universal themes

---

[24] See Tariq Ayubi, *Mufakkir i-Islam Sayyid Abul Hasan Ali Nadwi: Apne Afkār ke A'ine me*, 448-57.

[25] Ibid., 451.

[26] Ibid., 454.

of peace and harmony.[27]

If the *Payām* had a national purpose and appeal, Shaykh Nadwi's impassioned address to the Muslim community pointed to its moral responsibility in a multireligious and multicultural context. Shaykh Nadwi argued that the future of Muslims should not veer out of its Ibrahimi moorings. If, however, Muslims showed apathy towards protecting their collective identity, then there were bleak prospects of turning the volatile political tide in their favour. The following verse is a conclusive evidence of Islam's future in the country:

"Were you present when death appeared before Ya'qub? Behold, he said to his sons: What will you worship after me? They said: We shall worship your God, the God of your fathers – of Ibrahim, Isma'il and Ishaq, the One True God, to Him we bow [in Islam]." (2:133)

For Prophet Ya`qub, the most important issue was "the preservation of the faith of his children, their thorough grounding in faith and their adherence to true faith until their last breath." Shaykh Nadwi recounts this event for a variety of considerations. The main question raised is as follows: Have the Muslims safeguarded the faith of their children and future generation in a land dominated by polytheism? Again, the success of Muslims' future hinges on the absolute reaffirmation of faith.[28] Notwithstanding the challenges affecting them, Muslims are reminded of their commitment to their Ibrahimi faith and culture. In sum, Shaykh Nadwi highlights the universality of the Qur'anic ideals and realities embodied in the lives of the Prophets.

In a global context Shaykh Nadwi adds new dimension to the Qur'anic term *furqān*[29] as a beacon of hope for Muslims living under different political situations. *Taqwā* is usually translated as fear or piety. However, in the Qur'anic terminology it is much more comprehensive and revolutionary in its content. It covers beliefs and practices, aims and code of life sanctioned by Allah. If a believer is infused with the true spirit of *taqwā*, then Allah grants him *furqān* (distinctive characteristic or criterion) which permeates his whole being... By his exemplary conduct, he obeys the

---

[27] Bilal Abdul Hayy Hasani, *Sayyid Abul Hasan Ali Nadwi's Thought and Mission*, 186.

[28] Nadwi, *Guidelines from the Holy Qur'ān*, 257.

[29] "Believers! If you fear Allah He will grant you a criterion and   will cleanse you of your sins and forgive you. Allah is the Lord of abounding bounty (8: 29)."

dictates of Allah and His beloved Holy Prophet (peace be upon him). He is a well-wisher of humanity; he is a disseminator of guidance; he is a perfect human being who is virtuous, who keeps his eyes lowered, his tongue guarded and his mind free from evil plots and schemes – such a person possesses distinctive characteristics.

Shaykh Nadwi references this Qur'anic term to the earlier generations of Muslims who were the true embodiment of virtue and altruism. These pure-hearted souls were able to change the religious landscapes of countries. Their inspiring conduct rooted in the Islamic ethos succeeded in establishing vibrant Muslim communities in a short period of time. Their example can be replicated today if Muslims follow the Qur'anic message contained in the following verse:

"Oh you who believe, enter into Islam completely... (2: 208)."[30]

Conclusion

A holistic presentation of Shaykh Nadwi's multidimensional personality reveals interesting insights into various strands of Islamic thought that have helped shape the destiny of the *ummah*. No scholar can ignore the winds of change brought about by the twin concept of *islāh* and *tajdīd* which are conceptualised as a frame of reference for Islamic resurgence.

The contribution of Shaykh Nadwi to the field of Qur'anic studies delineates his reformist vision. The frontiers are expanded to enable a conversation with the myriad of issues affecting the *ummah*. Shaykh Nadwi is among the pioneering scholars to initiate a discourse without compromising the Islamic principles. His study of the Qur'an was extensive, as is evident from his famous works. However, his scholarly output has been downplayed by assertions that his historical expertise overshadowed his knowledge of *tafsīr*. In recent years, several theses and dissertations have contradicted this assertion. Interestingly, these writings adopt a hermeneutical approach in keeping with accredited academic standards.[31] Qur'anic studies since his demise in 1999 have made rapid strides in academia. The spate of writings covers a wide terrain of multidisciplinary knowledge that reaffirms the universality of the Qur'anic teachings and

---

[30] Nadwi, *Kārwān i-Zindagi*, vol. 7, 257-64.

[31] For example, the multivolume *Saviours of Islamic Spirit* received the Sultan Hasan Bolkiah prize in recognition of its rigorous historical standards in 1998.

message. Muslim scholars too, have made noteworthy contributions to the diverse subgenres of *tafsir*. Additionally, they have produced multivolume works that are reflective of impressive scholarship. Likewise, there is incremental interest to the growth and development of *tafsīr* amid the search for authentic translations of the sacred text. This trend augurs well for a robust, critical engagement with new methodologies and approaches.

The present study is intended to provide a forum for further research on Shaykh Nadwi's significant contributions to Qur'anic studies.

Bibliography

- Choughley, Abdul Kader, *Sayyid Abul Hasan Ali Nadwi: Life and Works,* New Delhi, 2012.

- Choughley, Abdul Kader, *Islamic Resurgence: Sayyid Abul Hasan Ali Nadwi and His Contemporaries,* New Delhi, 2011.

- Daryabadi, Abdul Majid, *The Glorious Qur'an: Text, Translation and Commentary,* Leicester, 2008.

- Ghazali, Muhammad, *The Sociopolitical Thought of Shah Wali Allah,* Islamabad, 2001.

- Hermansen, Marcia, *The Conclusive Argument of God,* Islamabad, 2003.

- Ismail, Abu Rabi, *Intellectual Origins of Islamic Resurgence in the Arab World,* New York, 1996.

- Khan, Shams Tabriz, *Tarikh Nadwat al-'Ulama,* Lucknow, 1984.

- Kidwai, Abdur Raheem, *Translating the Untranslatable,* New Delhi, 2011.
    - *From the Darkness into Light. Life and Works of Mawlana Daryabadi 1892 - 1977,* Springs 2013.

- Miftahi, Muhammad Zafiruddin, *Hayati-Mawlana Gilani,* Karachi, 1994.

- Mir, Mustansir, *Coherence in the Qur'an,* Indianapolis, 1986.

- Nadwi, 'Abdullah 'Abbas, *Mir Karwan,* New Delhi, 1999.

- Nadwi, Bilal Abdul Hayy, *Mawlana Shaykh Abul Hasan Nadwi's Life and Thought* (unpublished).

- Nadwi, Mohammad Akram, *Shaykh Abul Hasan Ali Nadwi: His Life and Works,* Batley, 2013.

- Nadwi, Muhammad Rabey, *Syed Abul Hasan Ali Nadwi: An Eminent Scholar, Thinker and Reformer* New Delhi, 2014.

- Nadwi, Sayyid Abul Hasan Ali, *A Misunderstood Reformer*, Lucknow, 1979.
  - *Da'wah in the West: The Qur'anic Paradigm*, Leicester, 1992.
  - *Faith versus Materialism*, Lucknow, 1976.
  - *From the Depth of the Heart in America*, Lucknow, 1978.
  - *Glory of Iqbal*, Lucknow, 1973.
  - *Guidance from the Holy Qur'an*, Leicester, 2005.
  - *Inviting to the Way of Allah*, London, 1996.
  - *Islam and Civilisation*, Lucknow, 1986.
  - *Islam and the World*, Lucknow, 1974.
  - *Mankind's Debt to the Prophet Muhammad*, Oxford, 1992.
  - *Meri 'Ilmi wa Mutala'ati Zindagi*, Rae Bareli, n.d.
  - *Puran i-Charagh*, 3 volumes, Lucknow,1984.
  - *Religion and Civilisation*, Lucknow, 1975.
  - *Saviours of Islamic Spirit,,* 4 Volumes, Lucknow, 1990.
  - *Stories of the Prophets*, Lucknow, 1976.
  - *Studying the Glorious Qur'an: Principles and Methodology*, Leicester, 2003.
  - *Ta'meeri-Insaniyat*, Karachi, n.d.
  - *The Role and Responsibility of Muslims in the West*, Leicester, 1993.
  - *Western Civilisation, Islam and Muslims*, Lucknow,1974.

- Peterson, Jakob Skovgaard, *Global Mufti: The Phenomenon of Yusuf Al-Qardawi*, London, 2009.

- Qardawi, Yusuf, *Shaykh Abul Hasan Ali Nadwi Kama 'Araftuh*, (Arabic) Damascus, 2001.

- Qutb Sayyid, *In the Shade of the Qur'an*, 18 volumes, Leicester 1999-2001.

- Usmani, Muhsin, *Mutala'at Tasnifat-i-Sayyid Abul Hasan Ali Nadwi*, Delhi, 2002.

- Wasey, Akhtarul and Kidwai, Abdur Raheem (ed.), *Journey of Faith: Maulana Abdul Majid Daryabadi,* New Delhi, 2016.

- Zaman Muhammad, *The Ulama in Contemporary Islam: Custodians of Change*, Princeton, 2007.